Advance Praise for

"*Love Cycles, Fear Cycles* is deceptively simple, powerful, and practical. It's readable, clear and straightforward. Yet it has the power to transform your relationship."

—TERRY REAL, LICSW

Author of *The New Rules of Marriage* and *How Can I Get Through to You?*

"*Love Cycles, Fear Cycles* is the core polarity that embraces all couples and deter-mines the quality and durability of their relationship. The authors skillfully use their relationship as the backdrop and illustration of negotiating that journey, producing an amazingly accessible book for all couples."

—HARVILLE HENDRIX, PhD, AND HELEN LAKELLY HUNT, PhD

Authors of *Getting the Love You Want* and *Making Marriage Simple*

"I think this is a very helpful book. Easy to read. Easy to understand. Easy to apply with or without professional involvement. Many a relationship will be made better and more rewarding because of Woodsfellow's insights and the openness with which he shares them. I highly recommend this book."

—MARSHALL DUKE, PhD

Charles Howard Candler Professor of Psychology, Emory University

"For those of you who are in a relationship and both love and struggle with your partner, this book will provide a thoughtful framework for how to ease your struggles. David and Deborah Woodsfellow share a personal story of love and working with that love to optimize it. They share a simple model for discovering ways to make your own love story better. This is an easy read that will provide insights for those who want to love more."

—DEBORAH BUTLER, PhD

Clinical Associate Professor, Robinson College of Business, Georgia State University

"The social world is based on relationships. Good ones and bad ones. Isolation is not the answer. Sometimes we fear, sometimes we love, and always we strive to find balance. This book provides the tools to create strong relationships and to understand our interactions with our partners. I appreciate the expertise of David and. Deborah Woodsfellow who guide us through a journey toward good bonds in life."

—RABBI DR. ANALIA BORTZ, MD
Congregation Or Hadash, Atlanta, Georgia

"I love it. This is a very sophisticated synthesis of attachment and other relationship theories and research, with well-validated approaches to behavior change, all presented in straightforward language. The examples make the concepts come alive and provide a strong foundation for discussion."

—NANCY BLIWISE, PhD
Professor, Department of Psychology, Emory University

LOVE CYCLES,
FEAR CYCLES

LOVE CYCLES, FEAR CYCLES

Reduce Conflict and Increase Connection in Your Relationship

DAVID WOODSFELLOW, PhD

DEBORAH WOODSFELLOW, MPH

SelectBooks, Inc.

New York

This edition published by SelectBooks, Inc.
For information address SelectBooks, Inc., New York, New York.

First Edition

ISBN 978-1-59079-440-1

Library of Congress Cataloging-in-Publication Data

Names: Woodsfellow, David, author. | Woodsfellow, Deborah, author.
Title: Love cycles, fear cycles : reduce conflict and increase connection in your relationship / David Woodsfellow, PhD and Deborah Woodsfellow, MPH.
Description: First Edition. | New York : SelectBooks, Inc., [2017] |
Includes
index.
Identifiers: LCCN 2017028132 | ISBN 9781590794401 (pbk. : alk. paper)
Subjects: LCSH: Interpersonal relations--Psychological aspects. | Conflict management. | Love. | Fear.
Classification: LCC BF1045.I58 W66 2017 | DDC 153.6--dc23 LC record available at https://lccn.loc.gov/2017028132

Book design by Janice Benight

Manufactured in the United States of America
10 9 8 7 6 5 4 3 2 1

This book is dedicated to our parents, who gave us the experiences that made us who we are and helped us understand the principles in this book. They each, in their own way, did the best they could, given the circumstances they faced. They each did wonderfully well at some things.

Thank you to
Norma and Gerson
Barbara and Don

CONTENTS

ᴧ

PREFACE

This book was written to help you better understand your close relationship. We hope you'll be able to see what's been going wrong for the two of you—and learn how to make things right. We've noticed a pattern that seems to be true of all partnerships. Commonly called vicious cycles, they are times when things get worse and worse, and you can't stop it. These cycles can result in bad fights, or in distance and withdrawal. Each person is part of these cycles; you do them together.

We hope that with the help of this book you'll learn to see your own cycles clearly. We hope you'll also learn to see what each of you does wrong, and the vulnerabilities that drive you. When you can identify these patterns, you'll have taken an important step toward making things better.

Then we'll talk about how to change your cycle. We hope you'll see the specific behaviors you each need to change, and the specific feelings that make each of you so vulnerable. We hope you'll also see how your past has contributed to your cycle. And we hope you'll be able to clarify what you truly want instead.

HOW TO USE THIS BOOK

If you want to explore this book in more detail, you might try the 24 exercises in the back. Most chapters refer you to particular exercises at the point when they might be most helpful. The exercises and the chapters cover the same topics, in the same order.

It's important to consider these ideas by thinking about what happens in your own relationship. If you're not in a close partnership now, consider your most recent or most significant relationship. These ideas come to life when you fit your own relationship into the general patterns we are describing.

Some people do that as they read; others benefit most by doing the exercises. If you're reading a chapter and something doesn't make sense, try the exercises. If you're working on the exercises and something doesn't make sense, try going back to that chapter. The chapters explain the ideas much more fully, and give you examples for comparison. The exercises guide you step-by-step through questions about your own relationship.

We've written the book for an individual to think about these things, and then apply them to his or her relationship. However, you might also want your partner to read this book, and talk about it together. If your partner is willing to do so, that might be wonderful. If they're not willing, don't force it. Just try it yourself for a while. Or, maybe a therapist might help.

There are a number of times in the book where we refer to getting professional help. See the appendix for those suggestions. If you are presently in therapy, you might want to share insights from the book with your therapist. It might be useful to see what they think about any new ideas you develop. This book is not a substitute for therapy. There are various problems for which no book can be adequate treatment. Consulting qualified professional therapists may be necessary to solve the difficulties in your relationship. While this book might supplement your therapy, it is not designed to replace it.

In the beginning of the book we talk more about fear, and in the end we talk more about love. Don't forget to focus on what you want. One part of making dreams come true is keeping your eyes on the prize. We wish you love and happiness.

ACKNOWLEDGMENTS

My wife, Deborah Woodsfellow, and I have lived this book together. We've studied couples therapy hand-in-hand for twenty-five years, going to workshops and trainings all around the country. We've used these ideas in our marriage; we've learned which work and which don't, which are hard and which are easy. We've developed ways to use this knowledge to help other couples. Together, we founded the Woodsfellow Institute for Couples Therapy. Our mission is to help couples save their marriages—and help therapists help couples. We've co-taught scores of workshops to therapists who want to learn more about couples therapy.

I did all the writing of the book, so whatever is lacking in the presentation is mine. But Deborah and I developed these ideas together through years of collaboration, so whatever is useful in this book is ours.

Deborah has also been a wonderful wife and extremely supportive collaborator throughout our working lives. She is thoughtful and intuitive, has remarkable insight into people, and a wonderful ability to convey ideas with simple, humorous, warm examples. She is great fun to work with, and great fun to build a life with. I have benefitted immensely from both.

Over the last twenty-five years we have studied with five leading authorities in couples therapy. We greatly appreciate their work and their insights. We have studied each of their approaches and worked to synthesize them. This synthesis is the basis of our clinical work, our teaching, and this book.

Dr. Harville Hendrix was the first person with whom we studied couples therapy. Harville taught that the deepest healing comes from the partner, not the therapist. That inspired me to start a practice of 100 percent couples therapy. Since 1992, my professional practice has been exclusively couples.

We learned many important lessons from Harville. One was that the "power struggle" is an inevitable part of all relationships, and that every couple's power struggle is a reflection of each person's unfinished business from childhood. He taught us that everyone has to deal with his or her greatest fear in the course of a marriage. This is not a sign of a bad relationship; it's the road to healing and growth for both partners.

Our second teacher of couples therapy was Dr. John Gray. He taught us the crucial importance of understanding differences between people. His use of humor to promote acceptance and coop- eration was extraordinary. He taught us ways to reframe some of the problems between couples in ways that people found easy to remem- ber. One classic was the difference between Martian "solving" and Venusian "understanding." We benefitted from learning to distin- guish the two—and so have hundreds of the couples we've helped.

Drs. John and Julie Gottman introduced us to couples therapy based on scientific findings about relationships. They taught us about the crucial importance to all couples of stability, friendship, conflict management, and a sense of meaning. We learned how to assess each of these and how to help couples build the ones that needed improve- ment. They helped us adopt a much more thorough way of beginning couples therapy that allowed us to quickly learn a lot about a couple so we could offer specific feedback about their strengths and weak- nesses and a detailed treatment plan for how to improve their mar- riage. This added important thoroughness, clarity, and concreteness to our work with couples.

Terry Real taught us how to work with difficult couples. Many people seeking help are not in easy situations. Not everyone does the things their partner suggests to improve a relationship, or the things we recommend. Terry has mastered how to work with these people. His concept of leverage was a crucial idea for us. He understands that therapists alone have little leverage to get people to change. Real leverage can only come from the client's own world—from their spouse, their children, their work, or something they care about deeply. Terry's ability to understand a client's genuine motivation, and use that for their benefit, is a profound gift.

Our most recent teacher has been Dr. Sue Johnson. She has taught us the importance of focusing on people's deep need for attachment. She's explained how to help clients get in touch with their underlying emotions and how to create moments for couples to share these feelings with one another. She teaches a model of human relationships that connects each person's feelings, thoughts, and actions in an interactive cycle that flows back and forth between the two people. Although her model differs somewhat from ours, it shares many important features and confirmed for us the utility of a universal model of relationships.

Regarding the writing of this book, we're indebted to Robyn Spizman, best-selling author and media expert, who helped us to turn this this project from an idea to a manuscript and also helped us to find an agent. Her energy, support, connections and know-how were all crucial. Her passion for people and ideas are extraordinary, and her knowledge of writing, promoting, and publishing has been very useful. She successfully guided us through much unknown territory. We could never have done this project without her.

Jackie Meyer, our agent at Whimsy Literary Agency, believed in this book and never stopped trying to find us the right publisher. Extremely quick-witted and insightful, her suggestions about various aspects of the project have been very helpful. Jackie is quite gifted at seeing different people's perspectives and working thoughtfully to promote collaboration. She's also made me laugh out loud with the connections she has seen between different ideas and how to best present them.

We are extremely grateful to Lenore Skomal, our editor at Whimsy, for wading through a pretty rough first draft and giving us some serious feedback that led to major rewrites. I appreciate her patience, her clarity, and her willingness to be honest with me about what worked and what didn't.

We appreciate Kenzi Sugihara and the entire staff at SelectBooks, Inc. for believing in our project. They made this book a reality—and created its actual manifestation. Nancy Sugihara and Molly Stern are wonderful, perceptive editors who have improved this book immeasurably.

A number of colleagues reviewed the manuscript and generously offered their comments. These include Dr. Ted Ayllon, Dr. Howard Maziar, Rabbi Dr. Analia Bortz, Dr. Deborah Butler, Dr. Marshall Duke, and Dr. Harville Hendrix. We appreciate their interest, their support, and their wisdom.

We are so grateful to all of the clients who allowed us into their lives at crucial moments of difficulty. We have been inspired by their courage and their openness. We have been humbled by their challenges. They've each taught us part of what it means to be human. No two couples are the same; each has their unique struggle. We've tried to learn from every one. This book is a synthesis of that learning.

INTRODUCTION

Intimate relationships offer us our deepest security, strongest friendship, most important teamwork, and best support for our dreams. But these relationships can also be frustrating. Almost every intimate relationship has good times and bad. Very few people are happy all the time in their long-term relationship. This is because relationships have "love cycles" and "fear cycles." In love cycles we feel wonderful; in fear cycles we feel awful.

Most relationships begin in a love cycle. You each feel good and made your partner feel good. It's lovely to feel happy and content, safe and secure. But over time most relationships also develop a fear cycle. That's the opposite of being in a love cycle—you each feel bad and make your partner feel bad. You wind up feeling unhappy and discontent, unsafe and insecure. In our love cycles we feel wonderful; in our fear cycles we feel awful.

There's a simple way to tell which cycle you're in now: you know by the way you feel. When your relationship feels good, you're in a love cycle. When your relationship feels bad, you're in a fear cycle. Or, perhaps, like many couples, you go back and forth between these two cycles.

In our work with thousands of couples we've discovered that all the love cycles of their relationships can be described in four words, and every fear cycle has another four words that can be used to explain what happens. This book, *Love Cycles, Fear Cycles,* will help you discover what these words are for the cycles of your relationship. The four words of your fear cycle will show you what's gone wrong, and the four words of your love cycle will show you how to make things right.

Your words are unique; they're not the same as everybody else's, because they fit your unique relationship. In your love cycle there is one word for each person's best feeling, and one word for each person's best behavior. In your fear cycle there is one word for each person's worst feeling, and one word for each person's worst behavior.

If you're in your fear cycle more than you'd like to be, this book is for you. A healthy relationship has a lot less fear and a lot more love.

Changing fear cycles to love cycles is the most important part of relationship therapy. Different therapists have different names for this, but they all address the same key task. Our Four Words method is the simplest, most straightforward and easy-to-use method we know. We developed it in the year 2000 and have taught this method to thousands of couples and hundreds of other therapists.

UNDERSTANDING LOVE CYCLES

There are four nice words in a love cycle and four not-so-nice words in a fear cycle. It will be interesting to discover your unique words.

I'll use our relationship as an example. When we met, Deborah was very talkative and outgoing. She explained her interest in ballroom dancing, and demonstrated with me right then. I thought, "Wow. Here's a woman who's really wants to be involved with me." I invited Deborah over for dinner and made my best dinner. I was very thoughtful, attentive and kind. She thought, "Here's a man who could cherish me."

Deborah was involved with me; I felt loved. I was kind; Deborah felt cherished. Feeling cherished made Deborah even more involved. Feeling loved made me even kinder. The four words in our love cycle were—and still are—kind, cherished, involved, and loved.

The diagram of our love cycle on the next page shows how these lead to one another:

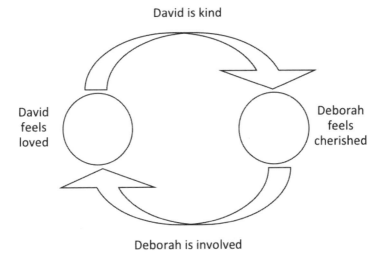

David is kind

David feels loved

Deborah feels cherished

Deborah is involved

Kindness leads to feeling cherished. Feeling cherished leads to being involved. Involvement leads to feeling loved. Feeling loved leads to kindness. The cycle goes round and round. It can start at any of these four places.

Deborah and I didn't know these words at the time, we just enjoyed being in love. It all seemed natural and effortless. The words in your Love Cycle will probably be different from ours, but they will also be caring actions and warm feelings.

DEFINING FEAR CYCLES

Unfortunately, relationships also have fear cycles. These happen when we feel scared, hurt, or angry. When you're in a fear cycle both of you feel bad, and react in ways that make the other person feel bad.

I remember talking to Deborah about our fear cycle very early in our relationship. I told Deborah what I thought could go wrong. As a therapist this seemed like a sensible thing to do—talk about a problem to prevent it. But to Deborah it felt much too soon to be talking about things like this. She thought, "Why is this guy anticipating the worst?" It was our first example of David's "let's-deal-with-this-right-now" and Deborah's "let's-deal-with-this-later."

I explained that if I got angry, that might make her fearful. Then she might withdraw, which could make me feel abandoned. That could lead to me getting angrier, and to her feeling more fear and withdrawing even more.

I figured this out from what I knew about me and what I'd learned about Deborah. I knew my greatest fear was abandonment, and my worst reaction to abandonment was getting angry. I knew other people didn't like my anger; so I guessed Deborah wouldn't either. Deborah had told me that as a little girl she been around some people who, when angry, had threatened to harm her. She had learned to withdraw as her first line of defense.

Although I'm not a physically violent person, I can raise my voice, and, in those days, I used to get loud when I was angry. So I saw how our cycle could develop:

David gets angry

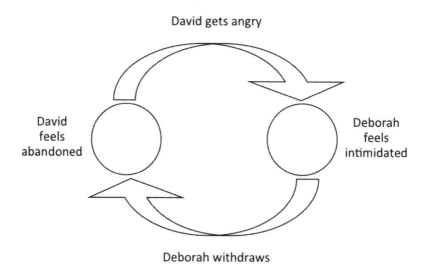

David feels abandoned

Deborah feels intimidated

Deborah withdraws

It turned out I was right. That was our fear cycle then, and it's still our fear cycle.

Your relationship also has a fear cycle. Your four words may differ from ours, but some kind of fight and flight, and some kind of hurt and loneliness, are part of all fear cycles.

CHANGING YOUR FEAR CYCLE TO A LOVE CYCLE

In this book, we'll help you identify the four words that best describe what happens in your fear cycle and your love cycle. The four words of your fear cycle reveal what's been going wrong. Each shows you something you'll want to change. Transforming your fear cycle back to your love cycle is the way to a wonderful, lasting relationship. It lets you live your dreams rather than your nightmares.

PART I

UNDERSTANDING YOUR FEAR CYCLE

CHAPTER ONE

WHY IS LOVE SO HARD?

CRISIS!

I was so mad I could scream. And in the old days I would have. Once again, Deborah had been unwilling to talk about something important. She kept putting it off, and I always had to bring it up again. As if I needed one more thing to remember! Looking back, I don't even recall what it was I wanted so much to discuss, but I sure remember how frustrated I felt.

I raised my voice. I wasn't yelling, but it wasn't my usual tone either. I said, "This is not okay! I can't keep living like this!" I said it strong and clear. No nonsense. I meant it.

That's when Deborah panicked. What she heard me saying was that I was threatening to get a divorce. She shut down. She stopped talking. She certainly wasn't going to tell me how she felt. She just walked away. We didn't talk for three days. We each seriously thought about leaving. It was a far cry from how we'd started.

SO RIGHT FOR EACH OTHER

At first we felt we were so "right" for each other. We felt we were *beshert*, a Yiddish word that means "meant to be" and came to mean "soulmate"—the one who completes and complements someone perfectly. We were both health care professionals; both early in our careers. We both liked to dance. We were both spiritual seekers, both interested in world religions, both interested in making the world a better place. Those similarities felt very important.

The two of you probably felt *beshert* at first. You sensed how well you fit together. You delighted in the things you had in common. You were thrilled by your shared interests and values; you loved discovering more of them.

You saw how you complemented each other. You loved your partner's different gifts. You saw traits you admired. You looked forward to having more of these in your life. I loved that Deborah was good with animals and plants; Deborah loved that I was a deep thinker.

You two probably felt pretty wonderful together too. You made each other feel very good. You were your best self—loving, caring, and giving—that made your partner feel good. In turn, your partner was loving, caring, and giving too—that made you feel very good. You two were in love.

This kind of connection feels fabulous. It's what we all want. It's thrilling and exhilarating, comforting and relaxing—all at the same time. The love resonates back and forth. That's your love cycle.

Our love cycle is sweet and simple:

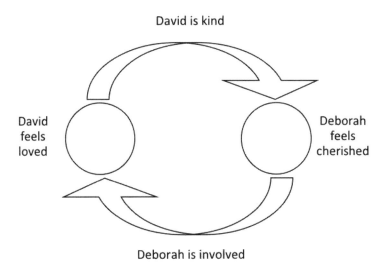

Each step leads to the next. Either one of us can start it. It just takes a word, a touch, a gesture, a glance.

You might think that love cycles like this should last forever; I wish they did. Unfortunately, the challenges and setbacks of life push us out of our love cycles. Our vulnerabilities and reactions push us out too.

SO WRONG FOR EACH OTHER

You and your partner aren't always so right for each other. Some of your differences don't feel good. You like to do some things that they don't; they like to do some things you don't. Some of your interests don't go well together. Sometimes, if they do what they want, you can't do what you want. That doesn't feel right.

Maybe they're a night person and you're a morning person. Maybe they like to save money and you love to shop. Maybe they're neater and you're more relaxed about things. Maybe they're very social and you're more of a loner. Maybe they like new things and you prefer old and familiar.

In good times, these differences are interesting and complementary, endearing and humorous. In bad times, they're frustrating and worrisome. They lead to arguments and disconnection. You might think, "How can they be right for me if they're so different?"

You're not alone; all couples have differences like this. These are not necessarily irreconcilable; you're not necessarily incompatible. There can be a healthy give-and-take. Differences can lead to creativity, flexibility, and growth—unless you get caught in your fear cycle. Then, compromise and collaboration don't work. Instead of making progress and feeling better, you get stuck and feel hopeless.

On our second date, we discussed our fear cycle:

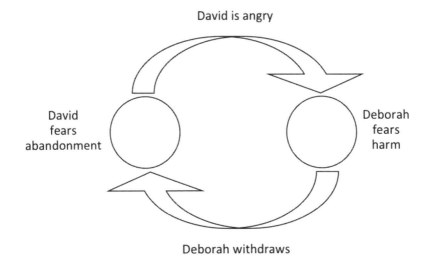

Deborah's greatest fear is being harmed. My greatest fear is being abandoned. These have been lifelong issues for each of us; they're our greatest vulnerabilities. When we feel these threats, things get bad—and our instinctive reactions make things worse. When Deborah fears being harmed, she withdraws. That's sensible. Who wouldn't pull back in the face of perceived danger? But her withdrawing triggers my fear of abandonment.

When I feel abandoned, I get angry. That makes sense too. Who wouldn't protest being abandoned? But my anger makes Deborah feel intimidated. Each of our reactions is the other's worst nightmare. When Deborah withdraws, I don't think, "Oh, Deborah's feeling scared, so of course she needs to pull back." I think, "Wait! Stop! Don't pull back! Don't leave me alone! We need to solve this! We need to talk about this right away!" My hurt and need are covered by my anger. My plea, "Don't leave me!" comes across as an angry attack. That anger drives Deborah further away.

When I get angry, Deborah doesn't think, "Oh, David's feeling abandoned. That's what he's so angry about." She thinks, "Danger! Danger! I need to get away!" Her plea, "Please calm down," comes across as withdrawal. That withdrawal makes me angrier.

In your fear cycle, each of you feels threatened and vulnerable. Each of you reacts in a way that threatens the other. It can escalate in a minute. It can keep going for hours. It can last for years.

To be happy together, you need to break out of that cycle. Your first step is to see it clearly, and understand the four words that describe it.

FIGHT AND FLIGHT

Animals respond to danger with fight or flight. People do too. When we feel threatened, we fight or fly. It's instinctive. If we think we can overcome the threat, we fight. If the threat seems overwhelming, we fly. Most people have a way they instinctively react. Some prefer fight; it comes more naturally to them. Others prefer flight. What's your preference? Do you usually fight or fly?

In this book, when we use the word "fight," we don't mean physical aggression. We mean any form of moving toward perceived difficulty. By flight, we don't mean literally running away. We mean any form of moving away from perceived difficulty. The movement can be physical or emotional, verbal or nonverbal.

Fighters speak up; they're not worried about conflict. They're willing to have difficult discussions. They let others know what they want. They move toward problems, not away. Fliers don't speak up because they don't like conflict. They don't want to hurt other people's feelings or be hurt themselves, so they avoid disagreements and arguments. They worry that discussions might make things worse; they're less likely to say what they want. They move away from problems, not toward them.

If you respond with "fight" more:

- You're willing to have conflict.
- You'd rather deal with problems right away.
- You believe that openness is the best way to solve problems.
- You accept the fact that sometimes people hurt each other's feelings.

- You like strong emotions; you think they're honest.
- At times, your partner thinks you are too confrontational.

If you use "flight" more:

- You don't like conflict.
- You'd rather deal with problems later, after things cool down.
- You believe that considerateness is the best way to solve problems.
- You think that people shouldn't hurt each other's feelings.
- You don't like strong emotions; you think they're dangerous.
- At times, your partner thinks you are too avoidant.

It's important to know whether you are a fighter or a flier, and which your partner is. You may already know this. If you're not certain, you might want to turn now to the exercises in the back of the book. These exercises are designed to help you apply these ideas to your relationship. Exercise 1 and 2 can help you confirm whether your style is fight or flight.

OPPOSITES ATTRACT

Most people are paired with their opposite. Most relationships are between a fighter and a flier. If you're a fighter, your partner probably prefers flight. If you're a flier, your partner probably prefers fight. In most couples one person is more talkative than the other. One is louder, the other quieter. One is more intense, the other calmer. One gets energized quickly, the other more slowly. You may already know your preference and your partner's. If you don't, exercise 3 can help you check whether you two are a fight/flight pair, or whether you have some other combination.

The world is fairly evenly divided between fighters and fliers. Neither is good nor bad; neither is better than the other. Each style is good for certain things and not so good for other things. Fight is good for problem solving; flight is good for peace. Fight is good for increasing intensity; flight is good for decreasing it. Each can be a strength; each can be a weakness.

In our relationship, I'm the fighter and Deborah is the flier. I like Deborah's peace and grace. I like her smooth, charming thoughtfulness. I like her ability to calm situations and make people feel understood. Deborah likes my strength and assertiveness. She likes my quick thinking and articulateness. She likes my ability to address things directly.

However, there's an inevitable difficulty between a fighter and a flier. When there's a problem, the fighter wants to talk right away, while the flier wants to calm down first. The fighter wants to engage, discuss, problem-solve, negotiate, and plan. The flier wants to delay, defer, consider, and take their time. The more the fighter pushes forward, the more the flier pulls back. The more the flier pulls back, the more the fighter pushes forward. These differences can be very frustrating.

WHEN OPPOSITES DON'T ATTRACT

Most couples have one fighter and one flier. But there are a few couples who are exceptions. Maybe you're both fighters or maybe you're both fliers. Or maybe you both fight and flight equally. A few sections of this book are especially for couples who are not fight and flight pairs. Exercise 11 will help you figure out a fear cycle that's not based on fight versus flight.

If you're both fighters, you believe that sharing your feelings is very important. You're emotional and passionate, but you can get really angry too. Your anger makes your partner angry, and vice versa. When you two fight, you have to be careful to not say things that could do emotional damage.

If you're both fliers, you're both cautious. You may not argue at all. You both tend to pull back at times of conflict. You believe in being careful and considerate, but you have to make an effort to talk about concerns so they don't become bigger problems.

Or, maybe you fight and fly equally. Do you fight about certain topics and fly away about others? Do you fight about children but take flight about finances? If so, these may be two different fear cycles. You might want to figure out your fear cycle about each topic separately. Or, do you fight and fly in sequence? Do you get angry first and then leave later? Or withdraw first and then get angry later? If so, you might want to figure out the fear cycle for "first" and the fear cycle for "later." They might be two different fear cycles.

IF YOU BOTH FIGHT

In some couples, both people fight. That can make a lot of conflict. Deborah and I aren't usually fight/fight, except on certain topics. I'll use one of those topics to give you an example of what fight/fight is like.

Charitable giving is one topic that makes both of us want to fight. We don't get nasty when we argue about charity, but we do disagree strongly. Neither backs down. We both believe in charity and we agree that we want to give 10 percent. So far so good. But we quickly bump into two problems. Ten percent of what? To whom?

Our marriage counseling business is the source of our income, but we argued about whether we should tithe our gross income or our net. At times our disagreement got pretty heated. I argued for gross; Deborah for net. I felt giving more was better while Deborah worried that we wouldn't have enough savings for our own security. I argued that in biblical days 10 percent of one's crops would have meant 10 percent of the gross. Deborah thought that argument was irrelevant and ridiculous.

Underneath this seemingly small question, there were deeper rumblings. I came from a well-off family while Deborah came from an impoverished one. My father, a surgeon, went to Harvard College and Harvard Medical School. My parents stayed married their entire lives. I went to excellent schools and my parents paid all my expenses through the age of twenty-one.

Deborah's father was a contractor, her mother a nurse, and neither had steady employment. In the beginning, they had a lovely suburban house with a pool in the backyard. But Deborah's parents divorced when she was young. After the divorce Deborah and her mother had very hard times. They moved frequently and were homeless one Chicago winter. There were months when Deborah didn't even go to school. At eighteen, Deborah joined the Navy so she could support herself.

My background was financially secure; Deborah's was extremely insecure. I didn't have to worry about money; Deborah still has nightmares of being on the streets.

We also argued about where our charity should go. I wanted to give money to Harvard. My father did, and I felt like I should too. Deborah thinks that's just plain wrong. To Deborah, charity means giving to people in need, not wealthy institutions. She wants to help people as directly as possible. Shelters, community food banks, and home building are the kinds of causes Deborah thinks we should support. Deborah and her mother wouldn't have survived without that kind of charity, and she wants to pay it back.

We argued pretty evenly about this, although Deborah was never the one to bring it up. I would raise the topic every December, as we tried to get our year's charity to align with our expected income.

I'd typically say, "Well, here's how we're doing so far this year. I think we've got about this much more to donate." Deborah would look at the list and say, "This is too much to give to Harvard. They don't need the money. And we're giving to your high school and the synagogue, too. None of those places need the money."

DAVID: Well I've committed to each of these amounts.
DEBORAH: Who cares! We don't have to keep those commitments.

DAVID: But I want to. My word is important to me.

DEBORAH: What about people who really need the money? We should be giving to them.

DAVID: Okay. I'm not against that. Who do you want to
           give to?

DEBORAH: Places that provide food and shelter.

DAVID: Okay. Let's give some to each.

Our conversation wasn't unreasonable. We give to a number of different organizations. We agree on how much to give in total. We each direct about half of our donations, and we talk until we have an agreement on all substantial donations.

But there were intense feelings underneath this healthy fight/fight disagreement. As I argued for what I wanted to do, Deborah took that as my demands. She felt controlled, like the decision wasn't hers to make. It seemed that money was being taken away from her, money that she needed. She felt that money was being used for unnecessary things while her need for security was being ignored. That's exactly what happened when her parents divorced. Her father didn't support her and her mother. He swindled them out of their home. He took things away that they truly needed. Our argument reminded her of all those years of insecurity and fear. In our discussions, Deborah felt those feelings again. She was upset, hurt, angry, and hopeless. I could see her hurt, terror, anger, and resentment.

Meanwhile, I felt criticized and unsupported. It seemed that Deborah was telling me what I wanted to do was wrong and bad. That didn't feel good to me. My mother had often been critical of my plans, so this stirred old feelings for me, too. Like Deborah, my mother was just trying to be helpful, but it made me feel unsupported. I remember, as a boy, that whenever I told my mother what I was going to do, she'd tell me what was wrong with it. Looking back I wish I could have focused on her helpful intentions and not been so defensive, but as a boy I just wished my mom would not be so critical.

In retrospect Deborah and I had a pretty healthy disagreement about charity. We each had legitimate points, and we each came to understand the other's position. We eventually came up with a compromise that felt okay to both of us. I had to reduce my gifts to some organizations, and it took me a while to get comfortable with that. Deborah had to get comfortable giving to institutions that she felt didn't need the money.

But our fight/fight process still evoked intense feelings that echoed each of our old hurts and fears. Here's a diagram of our fight/fight about charity.

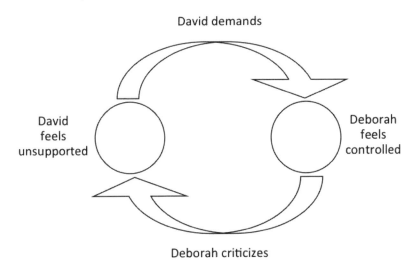

MOST OF THE TIME, FIGHT CAUSES FLIGHT

It's pretty easy to see why fight leads to flight. When one person gets angry or demanding, it usually makes the other person feel uncomfortable. Even with the best of intentions, intensity can seem threatening. It's instinctive for fliers to pull back. They need to feel safe more than they need to solve the problem. They need to get away from danger, especially when they feel as though they're outmatched. The quickest path to safety is getting away.

The more intensely I initiate a conversation, the more intensely Deborah withdraws. If I demanded, "WE NEED TO TALK RIGHT NOW!!!" she'd already be gone. There wouldn't be any conversation. It would probably take us a few days to recover. Luckily, I usually initiate conversations much more softly. Most of the time I say, "Honey, there's something I want to talk to you about. Is this an okay time?"

But Deborah still feels uncomfortable. She anticipates that I'm going to complain about something she's done. Before I've said another word, she's already in flight. I wish Deborah wasn't so reluctant to deal with problems, but she is. I can't change her instinctive feeling of fear; all I can do is make soft starts and less threatening conversations.

AND FLIGHT CAUSES FIGHT

If you're the flier, it might be hard to see how you cause your partner to fight. It might not make sense to you. You know that you're not doing anything to upset them—just the opposite. You're doing everything in your power to help both of you calm down. Why would anyone dislike that? You haven't said anything bad; you haven't said anything at all. That's the reason you avoid arguments, to avoid hurtful things being said. The last thing you want is an uncomfortable situation. So what are they so angry about?

Here's the answer: Your partner doesn't see avoiding an argument as a good thing; they see it as a bad thing. They see it as not fixing a problem that's keeping the two of you apart. They want you to talk to them. They don't want you to leave. Your flight just makes them feel empty and abandoned. This seems wrong to them, so they try to get you to change. They get demanding and angry because they feel abandoned.

Deborah and I have made some big progress here. These days, instead of saying, "I don't want to talk about it," Deborah says, "Let's talk about this later." That's progress. It's still frustrating to me, but it's not hopeless. We've come to the mutual understanding that: yes, we'll talk, but no, not at this minute. Deborah will talk, but she'll choose when. We respect my need to talk and her need to be prepared. With our compromise, we get both.

IF EACH OF YOU DOES FIGHT AND FLIGHT

Some people don't think of themselves as fighters or as fliers. They fight and fly equally—often one right after the other. Is this you? Do you begin with flight and then shift to fight, or vice versa?

For instance, I used to fight and then take flight. I'd get angry at Deborah and then storm off in a huff. I'd realize things weren't working, so I'd leave. Leaving isn't always a bad idea; sometimes stopping a conversation is the right thing to do. But I left unilaterally, with no warning. Deborah would feel criticized and attacked, and then, a moment later, she'd be alone with no resolution. There was no repair, no apology, and no agreement about what came next. This wasn't a good pattern.

Deborah used to fly and then fight, just the opposite of me. I'd want to discuss something and she'd say she didn't want to talk about it. I might bring it up again, and she'd say it wasn't a good time. She didn't suggest another time that would be better. There was no plan. I worried I would never get to address the problem, or not in time for a decision I needed to make. I'd bring it up again, and she'd get angry. She'd say, "I don't want to talk about this! Stop bugging me! Why don't you just let it go?!" She'd shifted from flight to fight. Now she was attacking me. In the first phase it was David fights and Deborah flees; then it became Deborah fights and David flees.

Perhaps you two reverse roles like we did. If so, you might want to consider your two phases separately. Try to understand the fear cycle in your first phase. See what you learn. Then go back and try to understand the fear cycle in your second phase.

CALLING TIME-OUT

Deborah and I have come up with a much better way of handling our fight-to-flight shifts. It's an agreement called "Time-out." It's a way to stop fight and flight—and to set the stage for a better discussion. Our time-out agreement goes like this:

- Either person can call time-out whenever they want.
- We do so by saying the words "Time-out," or by putting our hands together in a T.
- Time-out can be called for any reason. No explanation is necessary.
- When time-out is called, conversation stops immediately. Not another word is said.
- We walk away and go to separate places.
- There is a thirty-minute break.
- Both of us use the thirty minutes to calm down.
- Thirty minutes later we return to talk more reasonably and respectfully.

The key is making this agreement ahead of time, when you're calm, not in the middle of an upsetting situation. It's hard to negotiate an agreement when you're upset. When we have conflict, these agreements are already in place. Time-out works well for us.

These days, if I'm really angry, I call a time-out. Deborah knows I'm going to calm down. She knows I'll be back in thirty minutes. She has time to calm herself and prepare for the conversation. If I don't call a time-out, Deborah will. If she thinks I'm too angry, all she has to do is say, "Time-out." The intensity stops right then.

It's good to call time-out when you feel too angry to have a productive conversation, or when you think your partner's too angry to do the same. It's better to call a time-out before the anger gets too intense, before hurtful things have been said. Calling time-out too much is better than not enough. Calling time-out earlier is better than later. But calling time-out later is better than not calling it at all.

As you practice, it will get smoother. You'll call a time-out earlier and more easily. It's a very effective way to stop escalation.

MAKING APPOINTMENTS

We use another tool to help prevent escalation. We know that fighters want to talk about problems and fliers don't—that's a big difference. If you're not thoughtful about this, one of you will wind up chasing the other around the house. That's not good. Instead, I'd suggest making appointments when you need to talk about problems. This might sound funny, but it works very well. The rules about making an appointment are:

- Each of us can ask the other one to talk about any problem whenever we want.
- The other person either agrees to talk then, or picks another time they would prefer.
- That time must be within twenty-four hours.
- The one who suggests the delay is the one who initiates that next meeting.

This is a healthy compromise between the fighter's need to talk, and the flier's need to be prepared. Sometimes the talk happens right then; other times the talk happens the next day.

The one who wants to talk has to give up demanding and controlling the timing, but gets a guaranteed discussion. That person will have to be patient, but will get a more willing audience. The one who doesn't want to talk has to give up stonewalling, but gets to choose a time that works best for them.

WARNING: WHAT NOT TO DO

The most-basic diagram of a fear cycle shows the relationship between fight and flight.

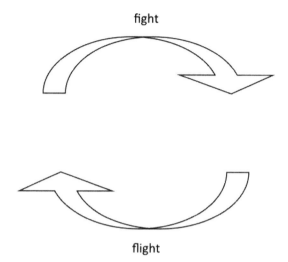

fight

flight

The lessons are from this diagram are:

- The more you fight, the more they fly.
- When they fly, don't fight—even though you feel like it. Fighting will only make them fly more.
- The more you fly, the more they fight.
- When they fight, don't fly—even though you feel like it. Flying will only make them fight more.

When Deborah seems to be avoiding something, my natural inclination is to discuss the problem and find a solution. But these days I don't push her to talk before she's ready. Patience is one key to our greater happiness.

In the past, when I was frustrated, Deborah would spot my irritation and withdraw. She'd move away so quietly that I didn't even notice. When I'd want to talk about a problem, she'd try to avoid the conversation. Her point was, "Don't make it such a big deal." Then I'd get agitated, and try to prove that we really needed to talk. The more intense I got, the more reluctant she got. We were off to the races again.

Now when I'm angry, Deborah does her best to walk toward me (not away) and say something (not be silent). She usually comments on some part of my point that makes sense to her. This works pretty well. I almost always calm down enough so that we can have a reasonable conversation. Being involved in problem discussions is another key to our happiness.

FREQUENTLY ASKED QUESTIONS

Here are some questions people have asked about fear cycles and love cycles:

Do all couples have fear cycles?
Yes. In the initial romantic love phase there may not be a fear cycle. But as time goes along, all couples fall into a fear cycle.

Are fear cycles nonstop?
No, fear cycles happen at certain times about certain topics. They may last minutes, hours, or days, but they don't continue nonstop. Other things eventually distract from the issue, and couples return to the business of ordinary life. But fear cycles will return at similar times or on similar topics in the future.

Do all couples have love cycles?
Yes. Most relationships start in a love cycle. That's the experience of being "in love." I believe that all couples can return to their love cycle. This happens when both people are feeling good and connected with each other.

↓ ↓ ↓

In chapter one you've seen how fight and flight make trouble in relationships. You've probably figured out whether you are a fighter or a flier, and which one your partner is. You've seen how fight and flight cause each other.

Fear cycles can escalate in minutes and go on for hours. In some relationships these fear cycles last years—or decades. No one wants this. In chapter two the different ways people fight and fly will be discussed—and the various feelings that result.

YOUR FOUR WORDS

The amygdala in the emotional center sees and hears everything that occurs to us instantaneously and is the trigger point for the fight or flight response.
                                        —Daniel Goleman, *Emotional Intelligence*

Most couples have one fighter and one flier. If this isn't true for you, I suggest that you think about specific situations in which you two do have a fight/flight dynamic. See what you can learn about your relationship from these times.

How Your Fighter Fights

Whether you're the fighter, or your partner is the fighter, how does this person fight? Try to find one word that describes it. Here are some possibilities. Does your fighter:

- get angry – use a raised voice or angry tone or intense words
- criticize – tell the other person what's wrong with them
- demand – tell the other person what they must do
- control – tell the other person what they can't do

Does one of these describe the fight in your relationship? If not, here are some more possibilities to consider. Does your fighter:

- yell or scream?
- accuse or blame?
- order or dictate?
- nag or pressure?

If your fighter does more than one of these, choose the one that's the biggest problem. If none of these words fit, use your own word.

If you're on the receiving end of the fighting, you can probably name this pretty easily. Deborah would say that my worst fighting is getting angry. She feels uncomfortable when I raise my voice. She doesn't like it when I tell her she's wrong, and she really dislikes my showing irritation with her when others can see it. She calls all these "getting angry."

If you're on the sending end of the fighting, it might be harder to see the worst part. You may be thinking about your good intention. You might be trying to solve the problem, but to your partner you might look demanding and not helpful. Sadly, your impact might be very different from your intention. To improve your relationship, you need to see your impact. Think about how your partner sees you. How would they describe your fighting?

Sometimes I don't think I'm angry. I think I'm just saying what I want. To me, that's not anger, it's reasonable assertiveness. But it seems pretty different to Deborah.

The worst kind of fight in your relationship is Word 1. It goes on the top arrow of you fear cycle diagram.

Word 1

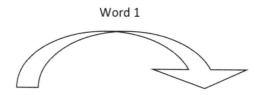

If you haven't been able to choose a word for this fighting, exercise 4 can help you find one.

HOW YOUR FLIER FLIES

Are you the flier in your relationship? Or is your partner? The flier is the person we'll be talking about in this section. The most frequent ways of flying are to:

- withdraw – pull back from the situation
- shut down – stop interacting entirely
- defend – explain why you are not at fault
- manipulate – use indirect methods to get what you want

Does one of these describe the flight in your relationship? If not, here are some other words you might consider. Does your flier:

- avoid or distance him- or herself?
- stonewall or ignore the other person?
- turn it around, and make it the other person's fault?
- play victim, and make the other person the bad guy?
- placate by agreeing, but then not follow through?

If there is more than one kind of flight, choose the one that's the biggest problem. Or do you have a different word for it?

If your partner is the one who flies, you can probably name their flight pretty easily. I would say that Deborah's worst flight is withdrawing. I get frustrated when she doesn't say anything. It's worse when she refuses to discuss something. Worst of all is when she gets silent right in the middle of a discussion. My word for all this is withdrawing.

If you're the one who flies, it might be harder to name the worst part of your flight. Maybe you only see your good intentions. Your intention might be to calm things down, but to your partner it looks like avoiding the problem. Unfortunately, your impact can be very different from your intention. Think about how your partner sees you. How would they describe your flight?

Often Deborah doesn't think she's withdrawing. She's thinks she's being thoughtful and careful. She doesn't want either of us to get upset. She doesn't want us to fight. She wants everyone to stay calm. To her, that's not avoiding, it's common sense. As you may imagine, it looks pretty different to me.

If you've been able to find a word for the worst kind of flight in your relationship, you've now named Word 2 of your fear cycle. Put Word 2 on the bottom arrow.

Word 1

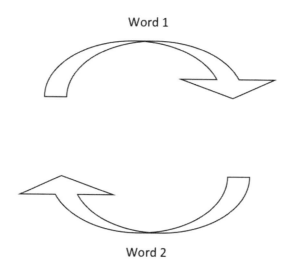

Word 2

If you haven't been able to choose a word for this flight, exercise 5 can help you find that word.

WORDS FOR YOUR FEELINGS

Just like there are many kinds of fight and flight, there are also many different feelings that follow. As we've reflected on thousands of couples, a few fundamental patterns have emerged. First, all these feelings involve some kind of fear. Second, there are of two kinds of fears: fear that something bad will happen, and fear that something good won't happen.

- Hurt and lonely are the two basic fears.
- Fear of hurt is caused by someone else's fight.
- Fear of loneliness is caused by someone else's flight.

ABUSE AND NEGLECT

The worst kind of fight is called abuse. It can create profound physical and emotional injury. Abused people have been harmed in ways that shouldn't happen to anyone. The worst kind of flight is called neglect. It involves profound loneliness and damage. Neglected people have lacked basic human needs.

In this book, we use the word "fight" to apply to normal behavior, not abuse. As used here, fight applies to people who are angry and intense, not people who are physically or emotionally abusive. We're proceeding with the idea that your partner, the fighter, is in the normal range of fight, not the abusive range. If you're in an abusive relationship, see Resources for Getting Professional Help.

Just like there are abusive fighters, there are also neglectful fliers. These people may want very little contact with you. They may have very few people in their lives. They may need their own space to an extreme degree. They might seem not to need warmth and connection. They can be extremely emotionally unavailable. We're proceeding with the idea that your partner, the flier, is in the normal range of withdrawal and avoidance, not the neglectful range. If your partner is severely neglectful, see Resources for Getting Professional Help.

IF YOUR PARTNER IS A FIGHTER

Fighters can feel scary—not scared-for-your-life scary, but still fear-arousing. When your partner is irritated, you definitely might feel uncomfortable. From your point of view, your partner is too angry, too intense, too demonstrative; and too talkative. They want to talk about feelings and they want to deal with problems. They want you to do these things too—and they want it right away. They talk too loud, stand too close, and go on too long. Deborah finds me too intense in these ways.

She often suggests I speak more quietly, and she's keenly aware of any other people in our vicinity. She cringes if I speak loudly, or gesture dramatically, in front of others. One time I was angry, and I shook my finger at Deborah. She was mortified.

Later when we talked about it, I discovered that she felt I was embarrassing her in front of other people. I had no idea what she meant. We were alone in our home. I said, "What other people?" She explained that we were standing by the window and neighbors could have seen us if they had walked past. I was amazed. That would never have crossed my mind. It wouldn't occur to me to worry about what a neighbor might think about how I spoke in my own house. But then, this wasn't even an actual neighbor she was worried about, this was a hypothetical neighbor—someone who might walk down our street. I had no idea she worried about such things.

From Deborah's point of view, I am wildly insensitive because I don't care about things like this. She dislikes that the possible repercussions to her, our neighbors and our reputation aren't my concern. Deborah thinks that I'm just focused on how I feel at the moment— and she's right. Those other things aren't on my mind.

This situation captured what she feared from a fighter. From her perspective, when I'm angry I don't care what damage I do. I don't care about other's feelings or sensitivities. I'm a bull in a china shop— who might break valuable, delicate items.

Fighters can appear to be thoughtless, careless, and rough. If you're with a fighter, you probably find them to be too intense and overwhelming. You probably wonder, "Why can't they just calm down and handle things more reasonably?"

Your Hurt Feelings

Fighters are hard to live with because their style can make other people feel bad. Their aggressiveness can come across as threatening. Even when they're trying to have a discussion or solve a problem, their energy can feel too strong. Remember the word you chose for how your partner fights. When they do this, do you feel hurt?

If the word "hurt" doesn't feel quite right, here's a list of some other feelings people have. Do you feel any of these?

- Attacked
- Bullied
- Criticized
- Scared
- Inadequate
- Controlled
- Powerless
- Overwhelmed
- Smothered

Does one of these words describe your feeling? If so, that's Word 3.

- Do you feel attacked or criticized or blamed—like they're pointing the finger at you?
- Do you feel controlled or powerless—like they're in charge and you're not?
- Do you feel scared or inadequate—like you don't know what to do?
- Do you feel inadequate—like anything you do will be wrong?
- Do you feel overwhelmed or smothered by their force and intensity?

If you need a different word, that's fine. If you have more than one word, pick the one that is most intense or most frequent. That's Word 3. It goes on your diagram like this:

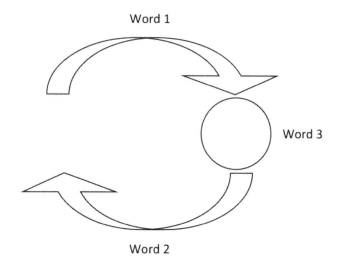

If you need assistance with this, exercise 7 can help you name your hurt feeling.

Your Partner's Hurt Feelings

If you're the fighter, can you see how your partner could feel hurt by what you do? I know it's not your intention to hurt them. If it were, you wouldn't be reading this book. But you still need to understand your impact, even if it's not your intention. It's not fun thinking about this, but it's important. When we're hurt and angry, many of us do and say hurtful things. Looking back, we have to understand how our partner feels about the things we do and say.

Remember the word for the way you fight. Think about how your partner feels when you do this. Put yourself in their shoes. What do they dislike about it? What's the hardest part for them?

You might not think of your reaction as fighting. Maybe you're just trying to explain your feelings, or trying to reach an understanding.

But you're coming across intensely, maybe aggressively. That's what your partner fears. Maybe they've told you this feeling many times. Or maybe they've rarely said it. Either way, you need to understand how they feel when you fight. That's Word 3.

If Your Partner Is a Flier

Fliers can leave you feeling all alone—at really tough moments. When fliers sense conflict or anger they pull back and stop talking. Sometimes they say, "I don't want to talk about it." Sometimes they just get silent. Sometimes they walk away.

It feels like they want to keep everything surface level. They seem unwilling to have serious, in-depth discussions. They don't want to know what you're feeling, and they don't want to share themselves too deeply. They think that talking about feelings is just going to make things worse; they want problem discussions to end quickly. You may find yourself in the position of trying to persuade them that talking is a good idea. It may seem that if you didn't keep bringing things up, problems would never get discussed.

You may have to persuade your partner that closeness is a good thing—because they're acting like it's not. You may know that they're "there for you" when it comes to loyalty and values, but you probably feel like they're not so present when you're upset. If you try to discuss this, it only makes things worse. The more concerned you are, the more they pull back. If you don't say anything, they're going to keep on withdrawing. If you do say something, they're going to withdraw because of what you said.

Your Lonely Feelings

Think about the worst way your partner flies. How do you feel when they do that? Does it make you feel lonely? Or is there a better word for how you feel? If you already know the answer, use that word. If you need some other suggestions, here some words other people have used:

- Rejected
- Unwanted
- Betrayed
- Abandoned
- Dismissed
- Frustrated
- Insecure
- Anxious

Do you feel one of these? If so, that's Word 4.

- Do you feel rejected, unwanted, and/or betrayed—as if they're saying they don't want you?
- Do you feel dismissed and frustrated—as if your feelings are not important to them and they don't want to hear them?
- Do you feel they're not here for you and you're on your own?

Is one of these true for you? Remember we're looking for your underlying feelings. Your first feeling might be anger, but see if there are other feelings underneath your anger. Most people get angry because they're hurt or scared. Is that how you feel? Or, is one of the above words right for you? Or do you have a different word for this emotion? Or, do you have many feelings? If so, see which one is the most intense or most frequent. This is Word 4. Here is where it goes on your fear cycle.

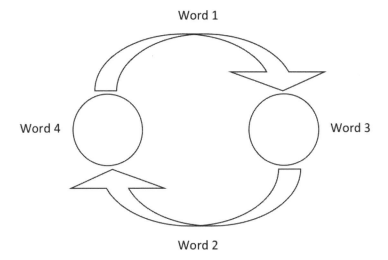

If you're having trouble naming this fourth word, exercise 8 can help you figure out these feelings.

Your Partner's Lonely Feelings

If you're the one who flies, your partner's loneliness may be harder to understand. You may not see your partner as someone who fears being lonely. You may see them as a strong person—a fighter—not a needy person. But many people hide their fear of loneliness under a show of strength. Your partner may do this.

You may be used to seeing your partner as the confident one. It may be hard to imagine the vulnerability underneath. But it's probably true. Angry people usually fear being left alone—even though they push people away. First they drive people away and then they get angry about being left alone. Sadly, most fighters have trouble seeing this. They see it the other way around: people leave them for no good reason, and then they get angry.

It might also be hard to see yourself as one who leaves. I understand that's not your intention. You just want to calm things down. You just want peace. You withdraw so that things won't get worse.

You're doing this to protect your relationship. But, sadly, when you withdraw, your partner doesn't feel protected; they feel lonely. I know you don't want to abandon them or make them feel lonely, but, when you pull back that's what happens. When you fly, they feel some sort of rejected and abandoned. That's Word 4.

🌱 🌱 🌱

The Four Words of Your Fear Cycle

In this chapter, you've seen how you each fight and fly. Fight usually causes hurt; flight usually causes loneliness. You've explored the particular hurt and lonely feelings you each have. You now have the four words of your fear cycle.

There is one word for:

- The way your fighter fights
- The hurt the other person feels
- The way your flier flies
- The loneliness the other person feels

These four words are the keys to saving your relationship. When you understand how these words flow into one another, you will be able to get out of your fear cycle when it starts, and stay out of it in the first place. If you need help putting your four words together, try exercise 10.

CHAPTER THREE

YOUR WORDS GO TOGETHER

If you want others to be happy, practice compassion.
If you want to be happy, practice compassion.

Dalai Lama XIV, *The Art of Happiness*

FIGHT AND FLIGHT COMBINED

Your fear cycle combines your fighter's worst way of fighting and your flier's worst way of flying. For Deborah and me it looks like:

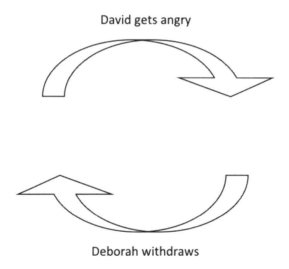

Can you see how your two words go together like this? If you're having trouble, exercise 6 can help you picture the combination of your two reactions.

Our diagram shows that anger causes withdrawal, and withdrawal causes anger. Your two arrows also cause each other. Here are some examples:

For fighters:

- The angrier you get, the more they shut down.
- The more you criticize, the more they defend.
- The more you demand, the more they withdraw.
- The more you control, the more they manipulate.

For fliers:

- The more you shut down, the more they get angry
- The more you defend, the more they criticize.
- The more you withdraw, the more they demand.
- The more you manipulate, the more they control.

All couples have some pattern like this. The details are different, but the interaction is the same. When fight and flight take over, you bring out the worst in each other. You threaten each other. You provoke each other's defenses.

THE SOLUTION THAT DOESN'T WORK

Your fear cycle is a problem you need to solve. But there's one "solution" that doesn't work—using your part of the cycle to correct theirs. This doesn't make things better, it makes things worse.

Yes, I feel angry when Deborah withdraws. I wish she wouldn't do it. I think it's not helpful. I don't like it. I think she does it too often. I'm angry because I think it's wrong. My feeling isn't unreasonable. But expressing that angry feeling would just make Deborah withdraw more, and that's the last thing I want.

When Deborah withdraws, she's trying to make things better, not worse. Her goal is to calm things down. She wants to make sure we don't get upset, hurt each other's feelings, or say words we'll regret. Those are good intentions, but her impact is the opposite. Her withdrawal makes me more upset, not less. We get nowhere with solving the problem; and I get angrier, not less angry.

Something like this is true for you too. When your partner does their part of your fear cycle, you'll feel like doing more of your part. But that response is not going to help. Don't do it. Your part in your cycle is an understandable response to what your partner does, but if you go ahead and do it right then, you're going to make the situation worse, not better. Your impact will be the opposite of your intention. There's a saying in therapy, "The solution is the problem." This is what it means.

HURT AND LONELY COMBINED

People feel hurt when something bad happens. People feel lonely when something good doesn't happen. These two are a pair. Hurt is the result of commission—when someone does something that feels bad to you. Loneliness is the result of omission—when someone doesn't do something that would feel good.

Hurt and loneliness fit perfectly with fight and flight. Fight is doing something that feels bad; flight is not doing something that would feel good. Fight is commission; flight is omission. In the same way that most couples have one fighter and one flier, most couples have one person who fears being hurt, and one person who fears being lonely. It's as if the flier is saying, "I'm okay with being alone, just please don't hurt me." And the fighter is saying, "I'm okay with being hurt, just please don't leave me alone." When things get really bad, these two happen at the same time. One of you feels hurt, while the other feels lonely. If you have trouble seeing how these feelings go together, exercise 9 can help.

Deborah and I experienced this about her "moving my things." I'm away from the house most of the day. Deborah is often home when I'm not. Sometimes she straightens up the house. That's lovely, most of the time. But a problem arises when she moves something of mine from its usual place to some "better" place.

That's not necessarily a problem. But it becomes a problem when I say, "Do you know where my so-and-so is?" Often she'll reply, "Look in the usual places!" with a tone that sounds irritated and conde-scending. It's as if she's saying, "Look in the usual places, you idiot!"

At those moments I feel angry—and left alone. I've already searched for the thing. I've already looked in the usual places. If it were in those places, I wouldn't be asking. I'm only asking because I'm pretty sure she moved it. Deborah doesn't mention that she might have moved it herself—and she's not offering to help me locate it. I'm on my own to find it. It's not a big deal, but it is a little moment of being alone.

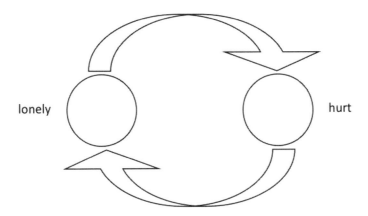

Meanwhile, Deborah thinks I'm angry at her for moving my things. This is scary to her. The last thing she wants to do is talk about it. She certainly doesn't want to admit any wrongdoing because she fears I might get even angrier.

I'm not mad—I just want to find the thing I'm missing. She moves things pretty often, and I'm just wondering if she knows where it is. But from fear of my anger, she leaves me alone with the search—and the conversation.

So, one day we talked about this. I explained that when I asked her where something was, I had already checked in all the usual places. I was really saying, "It's not where I thought it should be, and I'm wondering if you might have moved it." But I was trying to ask nicely, without anger and accusation.

I told her that in the future, I'd try to say, "I wonder if you might have put my so-and-so someplace," rather than just ask where it was. Then I requested that she try to remember that if I said, "Do you know where so-and-so is?" I meant "Could you possibly have moved it?" She said she'd try, and she's succeeded. Now she doesn't say, "Look in the usual place," when she's feeling, "Hey, I didn't move it. Don't start blaming me." Now she says either "I don't know honey; I haven't moved it," or "I might have moved it; let me check." Each of these responses feels much better to me.

These days I'm not accusing her, and she's not snapping back with an implied put-down. I'm asking a question, and she's helping me, either with information or assistance. Now we're working together— no hurt, no loneliness.

How Conflict Escalates

The worst thing about a fear cycle is that it escalates. You don't just provoke each other's reactions; these continue to worsen them. These four words lead to one another very quickly. You each feel truly threatened; you both get strongly reactive; and the threat keeps getting passed back and forth. It's the worst-case scenario of your two deepest fears and your two instinctive defenses—your own personalized perfect storm.

In a pursuer/distancer cycle this escalation is especially clear. Pursuing leads to distancing; distancing leads to pursuing. Pursuers make their partners feel smothered; distancers make their partners feel abandoned. Pursuers run after their partners to not feel abandoned. Distancers pull back from their partners to not feel smothered. The cycle on the next page shows what this looks like.

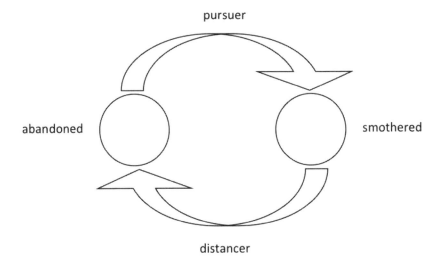

If you're the pursuer, you probably like to talk; your partner not so much. You ask them to talk; they say they're busy. You tell them it's important; they say it can wait. You urge them; they walk away. You follow them; they close the door. You complain; they tell you you're being unreasonable. You get angry; they lock the door. You beg; they ignore you. You pound on the door . . .

If you haven't gone this far, be grateful. But if you have gone this far, you understand escalation. If you've gone even farther, you know that escalation can get dangerous.

Escalation happens when you keep doing more of what you're already doing. If you're pursuing, and things aren't working, you pursue more. If you're distancing, and things are getting worse, you distance more. As silly as that sounds, it's amazing how much we do it.

Here's an example of pursuer/distancer in our relationship. I'm the pursuer, Deborah's the distancer.

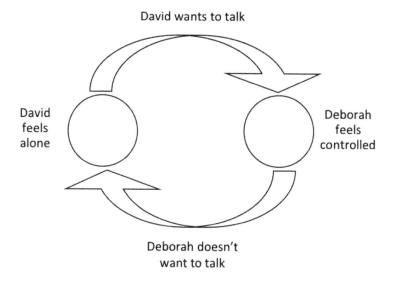

David wants to talk

David feels alone

Deborah feels controlled

Deborah doesn't want to talk

DAVID: There's a problem I want to talk to you about.

DEBORAH: This isn't a good time.

DAVID: When is?

DEBORAH: I don't know.

DAVID: Before dinner?

DEBORAH: I've got a lot to do today.

DAVID: Well you pick a time.

DEBORAH: I'm busy; I can't stop and figure that out right now!

DAVID: This isn't right. You're not being fair.

DEBORAH: Stop badgering me!

DAVID: You always do this! You always put things off!

DEBORAH: Why do you always badger me?!

DAVID: This makes me so angry!

DEBORAH: (Sighs and walks away.)

This is how our conversations used to escalate. They'd start with a request and a negotiation, but then quickly escalate to frustration, complaints, and criticisms. They would end with anger and withdrawal. We each felt bad; we each felt wronged.

The more I'd push to talk, the more Deborah would resist. That was sensible in a way. She would feel my intensity and get worried that a complaint was coming. No one likes complaints. But the more she put off our talks, the more frustrated and pushy I would get. That was sensible in a way too. Maybe she'd never agree to talk. These things were important; decisions needed to be made, problems needed to be solved. Our two sensible responses led us right into our fear cycle; and that wasn't good for either of us.

Thank goodness we now make appointments instead having this struggle. "Let's talk now" versus "let's talk later" doesn't need to be a fight. It's much nicer as a compromise. Our two different needs are respected much better without escalation.

How Couples Polarize

Polarization is a problem that happens more slowly, as the two of you develop opposite ways of doing things. If you're a parent you probably know the good-cop/bad-cop polarization. One of you is strict; the other lenient. You get stricter because your partner is so lenient, or more lenient because your partner is so strict.

When Deborah and I met, I was a single parent. Deborah thought that I was too lenient—and she was right. I didn't have a working system of responsibilities and consequences. I didn't have rules that worked. I was inconsistent. This was all true. Deborah tried to encourage me to be stricter and more consistent. These were good ideas, but they put her in the role of bad-cop.

Deborah didn't like this role, but she kept seeing me make the same mistakes, and was trying to help. I understood her point, but I kept making exceptions and excuses. Our polarization looked like this:

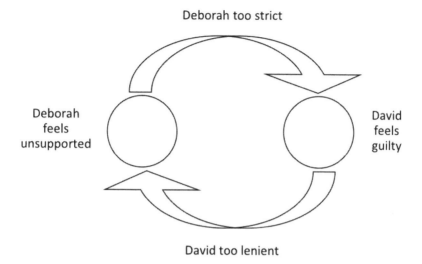

Not wanting us to be too strict, I wound up being more and more lenient. Not wanting us to be too lenient, Deborah wound up being stricter and stricter. When Deborah was strict, I felt guilty about being too harsh on my son. So I didn't implement our agreements very well. I let him slide too often. So, of course, Deborah felt unsupported. Here she was helping me with my son, trying to be a good parent, and I was undercutting her efforts. When Deborah felt no support, she got firmer. To me that looked like rigidity, and we were off to the races.

In balancing each other and compensating for each other, we both overdid it. Like with any polarization, we weren't our whole selves. Of course Deborah can be flexible and kind. Of course I can be firm and no-nonsense. But as we polarized, we weren't being those ways.

We fixed this by having a lot of "parent meetings" where we stepped aside from my son and talked privately about what we wanted to do next. We worked out compromises between us, and then announced them as our joint decisions. By closing ranks we reduced our polarization. It didn't work out perfectly—parenting rarely does—but we collaborated more and polarized less.

When any of us polarize, we miss our partner's wisdom. I didn't want to be harsh, but Deborah was right that I needed to be more firm. Deborah didn't want to be a pushover, but I was right that she needed to be more flexible. When we overcompensate for one another, we lose the virtues of the middle ground—like being firm and flexible.

Your Mutual Enemy

Your fear cycle is your mutual enemy. It can happen quickly. It can happen anytime. It brings out the worst in each of you, and it feels bad to both of you. You need to recognize this mutual enemy. You'll be better off when you learn to spot it early. When I need to talk to Deborah about a problem, I can already see how easily we could move into pursuer/distancer. The earlier you recognize your fear cycle, the easier it is to stop it.

If you can't see a cycle, you're probably just looking at your partner's wrongdoing. That's not likely to work out well. Try to notice how you're both involved. Be on the lookout for your fear cycle. Keep a careful eye out for your four words. Remember them. When you see any one of them, anticipate the others.

I tend to get angry when people withdraw. I do it with Deborah, and I've done it with other people, too. But I've noticed that my anger just makes people withdraw more. Even worse, they then say the reason they're withdrawing is because I'm angry. That really makes me mad. And then, of course, we're in a fear cycle.

I don't think I can change how I feel at those moments, but I can definitely change what I say and do. I've dramatically reduced how much I express that anger. Usually, I try not to express anything right away. Instead I pause to think about what would be best for me to do. Sometimes it's talking more calmly. Sometimes it's just allowing time to pass.

But I try hard to not express enough anger to give people more reason to withdraw. I understand how easily that could happen. I use this awareness to help me not worsen my fear cycles. If I can do it, you can too!

FREQUENTLY ASKED QUESTIONS

Do all couples have the same four words?
No, each couple has their own unique four words. Your words reflect your particular reactions and feelings. Your words might be the same as one of the examples in this book, they might be a variation of one of these examples, or they might be unique.

Are my four words the same as my partner's, or are they different?
They might be the same, or they might be different. You might have different perspectives on the same fear cycle, or you might be thinking about two different fear cycles.

What if our words are different?
If you have different perspectives on the same cycle, talk with each other. Try to come to agreement about a set of words you both can use. Listen to each other, understand each other's point of view, and see if you can come up with words that can work for each of you. It will be easier to change your cycle, if you can agree on how to describe it.

If you are thinking about two different cycles, discuss those cycles one at a time.

Are all problems circular?
No, all problems are not circular. There are some problems that are caused by one person alone. That kind of problem isn't a circle; it's a straight line. A causes B; but B does not cause A.

However, the vast majority of problems are both circular and not circular. Usually, part of the problem is mutual—and part of the problem is one person's fault. There may also be a part of the problem that is the other person's fault.

Some problems are more circular, some not so much. It's not all or nothing. If there is any circularity to a problem, each person's best strategy is to change their own part of that cycle. It's a very common error to think that a difficulty is "all your partner's fault." While that's not logically impossible, most of the time it's not true.

If a problem is circular, does that mean that no one takes responsibility for it?
No, the opposite: both people take responsibility for the fear cycle. Both start it, both keep it going. Neither takes all the blame for the past; both take responsibility for the future.

Are there four words or eight words?
Both. So far we've discussed the four words of your fear cycle. In Part II, we'll discuss the four words of your love cycle. These love-cycle words are the opposite of your fear-cycle words.

☙ ☙ ☙

In chapter three, you've seen how your four words describe an escalating cycle between you. This cycle is an opportunity for you, and a danger. The opportunity: If you can get out of your fear cycle, you can be happy together. The danger: if you can't get out of your fear cycle, you can't be happy together.

It's that simple—and that important.

CHAPTER FOUR

YOUR FEAR CYCLE

Named must your fear be, before banish it you can.

—Yoda, *Dark Lord Trilogy*

In this chapter we'll show you another method to figure out your four words. If you already have your words, this is a way to check them. If you don't already have your four words—or if you aren't a fight/ flight couple—this method may help. It will be especially useful if:

- You're both fighters
- You're both fliers
- One (or both) of you are neither a fighter nor a flier

What's the Worst Thing that Happens?

First, when things are bad between you and your partner—when you're not getting along or when you're arguing—what's the worst thing your partner does? Which of their reactions is most difficult? Which make things go wrong? You probably know this pretty well. It's what troubles you most about your relationship.

Try to capture this in one word or phrase. If they do a number of things you don't like, which is the worst? Your answer goes on the top arrow of the diagram. For instance:

He is selfish

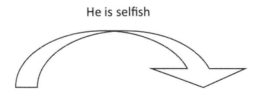

Second, when they do this, what is the worst way you feel? Do you feel surprised, upset, uneasy, or uncomfortable? What is your most troubling feeling? If your emotions are layered, try to get in touch with the deepest one. That's called your worst feeling and it goes on the circle to the right. For instance:

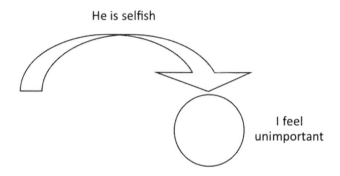

He is selfish

I feel
unimportant

The third question is harder. When you feel this way what is the worst thing you do? Anybody would react; I'm sure you do too. You need to name your worst reaction.

I'm not asking:

- What should you do?
- What do you want to do?
- What do you do on a good day?
- What is the best thing you could do?

I'm asking:

- What's the worst thing you do?

You're probably not proud of this, but you need to look at it clearly. Nobody's perfect; nobody does the right thing all the time. It's crucial to identify what you do wrong in these moments, because this reaction is what keeps your fear cycle going.

Put yourself in your partner's shoes. What would they say about you? What do they dislike? What do they want you to change? Maybe that's the worst thing.

For some people this isn't hard at all. They know exactly what they do wrong. They get too stubborn, manipulative, or defensive. But for other people answering this question is quite difficult.

It may hard to think that you are a part of the problem. Maybe your partner starts it. Maybe their part is worse. Maybe they did this long before you met. Any of these might be true.

But it's also true that you're doing something that's not working. Yes, you may have good reasons for it. Yes, it may be a reaction to what they do. But you're part of this dance.

Some people find this hard to admit. If your partner blames you and tells you it's all your fault, it can be scary to admit anything. You might worry that your partner would use it against you. Or, maybe all you can see is your good intentions.

Here's a classic example of good intentions but bad impact. Deborah is having a problem. I sympathize and want to be supportive. I let her know I can understand what she's going through, but then I suggest what she might do to solve the problem. That's when we get into trouble. The more I suggest, the more Deborah hears angry judgment. My intention is good, my impact is not.

Do you do something like that? Can you see what you partner doesn't like about your impact? It's difficult to understand how your impact may differ from your intention. But it's crucial. You may think you're doing one thing, while you come across very differently.

Or maybe it's just plain hard to admit any flaws. Maybe you can't see any bad in yourself. Perhaps you've been raised to think that you can do no wrong. That's a tough legacy, and it's going to make it impossible to see any circular pattern.

Or maybe you are convinced that all the problems in your relationship are your partner's fault. If this describes you, I've got something important to suggest. It might be hard to hear, but if you can't identify anything you yourself do wrong, maybe the worst thing you do is blame. Maybe your part of the cycle is blaming.

In a way, this is understandable. Your partner's reaction certainly makes you feel bad. Of course you don't like it, and want it to stop. Pointing this out could seem like the best way to get them to stop. But if they took this as blaming, that could make a fear cycle.

So it's crucial that you find something for this bottom arrow that you can genuinely acknowledge as a problem of yours. For example:

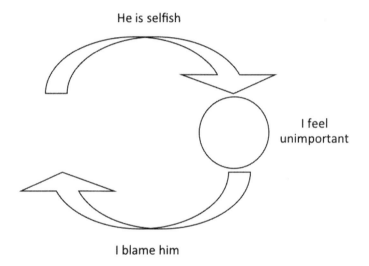

He is selfish

I feel unimportant

I blame him

The fourth question is also difficult. But it's the single most important thing to know about your fear cycle and about your partner. The question is: "When you react like this, what is the worst way they feel?"

What is the worst feeling your partner has in response to your worst behavior? Your reaction makes them feel bad, just like their reaction makes you feel bad. It may be something they've told you many times, or maybe it's something they've never told you.

This question requires empathy. You have to put yourself in their shoes and imagine what they might be feeling. You have to see yourself from their point of view. We're looking for their worst feeling—the most troubling, unpleasant, hurtful, threatened feeling that they have. If two feelings seem the same, go with both of them. If one seems deeper, go with that one.

I don't like to think that Deborah fears harm from me. It's certainly not what I want her to feel. I feel ashamed of her fear; I don't want anyone close to me to feel fear. But I have to admit that this is how she feels when I get angry. It makes me want to renew my commitment to not be scary, and to back off and apologize whenever my anger starts. It also helps me understand why she withdraws.

Your partner's feeling goes on the circle to your left. For example:

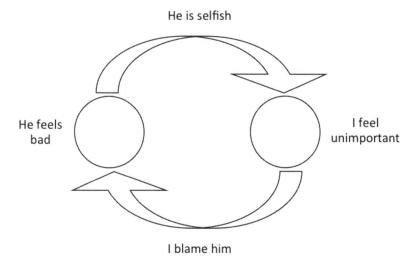

DOES IT ALL CONNECT?

Now that you have your four words, see if they make a cycle. Let's check all four links. We'll go around from the easiest- to- understand to the hardest. Exercise 12 also leads you through this process.

The easiest link to understand is from their arrow to your circle. Can you see how what they do leads to how you feel? Most people see this pretty clearly. I know that when Deborah withdraws, I feel abandoned. I also feel hurt and angry; but the deepest feeling is abandonment.

You may have heard that no other person can cause your feelings. There's some truth to that. The way you feel is determined by many factors—your perception, your thoughts, your life experience. But for practical purposes, Deborah's withdrawal is very often followed by my feeling abandoned. Does that mean her withdrawal causes my feeling? No and yes. No, it's not the only cause. No, it's not the inevitable cause. But yes, it leads to it frequently. And yes, it's the immediate cause.

The next link is from your circle to your arrow. Can you see how your feeling leads to what you do next? We're talking about your worst reaction, not your best reaction. When Deborah withdraws, I know I should be kind, patient and understanding. I know I should be quiet and give her time—and that's what I do on a good day. But in fear cycles we're talking about our worst reactions and our bad days. Everyone has worst reactions. You do too. If you're not sure about your worst reaction, think about your partner's complaints. I bet they know what your worst reaction is.

The next link is from your arrow to their circle. Can you see how what you do leads to their feeling? You need empathy to see this. You need to see that you threaten your partner in some way. You need to imagine how they feel at those times. Perhaps you wouldn't feel the same way, but empathy means putting yourself in their shoes, and those shoes are different than yours.

To see this link, for a moment you have to see yourself as the "bad guy" and your partner as the "innocent victim." Of course, that's not the whole truth of your fear cycle—but it's part of the truth. Some people have a lot of trouble seeing this link. It's especially hard if:

- You feel deeply wounded
- You think of yourself as an innocent victim
- You feel righteous indignation
- You blame your partner for the all the problems in your relationship

- You see yourself as right and them as wrong
- You see yourself as good and them as bad

Any of these may be true—perhaps more than one. But if these are all you can see, you won't be able to understand your fear cycle—and you won't be able to improve your relationship.

If this is where you honestly stand, it's probably time to get professional help. One of three things needs to happen. Maybe (a) you need to end this relationship; or (b) they need to seriously change what they're doing, or (c) you need to radically change your approach. I suggest you get help to figure out which of these is best, and how to do it. See Resources for Getting Professional Help.

The last link is the most difficult to see, but the most important. Can you see how their circle leads to their arrow? Can you see that when they feel this bad, they do the thing you like least? For me it's pretty easy to see how anyone who feels intimidated would withdraw.

I might be inclined to think that Deborah shouldn't feel intimidated. I'm not a bad guy, and I don't get very angry anymore. A little irritation on my face isn't such a big deal—there's no reason for her to get so fearful. I could say all those things to myself, but that wouldn't help me understand her. The trick is to understand the very thing I dislike—her withdrawal.

You need to do the same. You need to understand how your partner's reaction makes sense. You don't need to like your partner's reaction, but you do need to understand that when they feel bad, this reaction is what happens.

If this last link makes sense, you've understood your fear cycle. It explains what's been going so wrong between the two of you. It explains why you've been feeling so bad, and why things don't get resolved. It also points out what you need to change. The second half of this book will show you how to make those changes.

If this last link doesn't make sense, the next section may help.

WHAT IF IT DOESN'T CONNECT?

The harder links to connect are the ones on your partner's side of the diagram. If you're having trouble making those connections, here are some suggestions.

Consider whether your partner might have a deeper feeling that might explain the cycle better. If I thought Deborah was just irritated, her withdrawing wouldn't make that much sense. But when I realize that she feels intimidated, then withdrawing makes a lot of sense.

If it's a feeling they have mentioned before, use that feeling—even if you think they shouldn't feel that way. See if that feeling would explain their reaction. Consider fear, hurt, and loneliness. Might their deepest feeling be one of these?

Deborah didn't mention the word "intimidated" at first. She wouldn't have liked the word, because it sounded too vulnerable. She only shared this word at a time she felt very safe and secure. It wouldn't have come out at a time she felt threatened.

Think about the feelings your arrow might cause anyone. How might a very sensitive person feel? How might a very fearful person feel?

It's difficult, but you need to see how you can be challenging, difficult, or threatening. Of course, these aren't the ways you want to be. However, they may be the way you come across to your partner at certain moments.

You can also work backwards around the cycle. What feelings of theirs could possibly lead to their fight or flight? If they raise their voice, what feelings could lead to that? If they withdraw what feelings could lead to that?

Maybe the connection makes sense for your partner, even though it wouldn't make sense for you. If you were scared, you might not get angry, but maybe your partner does. If you felt hurt, you might not withdraw, but maybe your partner does. If you're still having trouble making all the links connect, try exercises 12 and 13.

WHO STARTED IT?

Many couples argue about who starts arguments. Maybe you two do this. Maybe you try to prove that your partner starts things. Maybe you give examples of how they have. Maybe you say they acted this way before you met them. Maybe you say this behavior comes from their family. Maybe they say these same things back to you.

Usually this kind of blaming isn't very helpful. Your fear cycle has gone around hundreds of times. Each of you has started it very often. Fighting about who started it this time just adds a second fight to the first.

Deborah could say she withdraws because I get angry. She could say that if I didn't get angry she wouldn't withdraw. Therefore, I start it. She could argue that no one likes anger, and anyone would want to stop anger before it gets too intense.

Deborah can sense my anger before I'm even aware of it. Sometimes I get a worried look, and my face can fall into a frown. Deborah senses my displeasure, frustration, or irritation, and it all seems like anger to her. She anticipates criticism, feels anxious, and then withdraws.

My perspective is totally different. I think she starts the cycle. Yes, twenty years ago I used to get too angry, but I haven't been angry like that for a long time. Yes, I sometimes feel angry, but I rarely express it with any intensity. There's not that much that makes me angry these days. However it's true that I don't like withdrawal. When Deborah avoids talking about something, or withholds information I need to know, it does make me irritated. If she didn't do this kind of thing, I don't think I'd be very angry at all.

Each of us could blame the other for starting it, and there'd be some truth to what we each said. But blaming would just create another fear cycle. First we'd be in a fear cycle about the problem, and then we'd be in another fear cycle about who started it. Blaming doesn't get you out of a fear cycle; it gets you in deeper. If you only see your partner's part and not your own, you're blaming.

At the opposite extreme, if you see only your own part, and not your partner's, you're placating. Blaming and placating are both big trouble, and they won't help you break your cycle. Instead of only seeing one person's part, you need to see how you're both in it together.

Here's an example of a problem Deborah and I solved by not blaming each other: Often when I'd talk to Deborah I would pause, expecting Deborah to reply. But she wouldn't say anything. There would be silence for a minute, then two minutes, then three. I didn't like that Deborah would end our conversations so abruptly.

I could have blamed her for withdrawing and stonewalling. She could have blamed me for getting angry and being impatient. We each thought these things, but, thank goodness, we didn't say them. Instead, we discussed the situation. Deborah told me she wasn't ending the conversation. She was just thinking about what she wanted to say next. She thought that was obvious. It sure wasn't obvious to me. But I was glad to know what was going on with her. It wasn't what I'd thought. Then we came up with a plan.

Now, at those times, Deborah says, "I'm thinking." That one little sentence helps a lot. I realize she isn't withdrawing; she just needs some time to gather her thoughts. So I don't get angry. Sometimes she'll forget, and make one of those long pauses, and not say anything. So I ask, "Are you thinking?" She smiles, appreciating my gentle reminder of our plan, and says, "Yes, I'm thinking." And we're good.

Perceptions and Misperceptions

Fear cycles are started by wrongdoing—and perceived wrongdoing. Each of you has done wrong. And each of you has perceived the other doing wrong. Sometimes that perception has been accurate, sometimes not.

I might not think I'm angry, but if Deborah thinks I am, we're off to the races. We've even had arguments about whether I'm angry or not angry. That becomes a fear cycle very quickly. I might say, "I wasn't angry before, but I'm angry now. I'm angry because you always think I'm angry when I'm not." That's pretty funny when you think about it—getting angry while arguing that you weren't angry a moment ago. But people do this all the time.

The bottom line is this: If you've discovered a genuine fear cycle between the two of you, then you've been around this cycle hundreds of times. It has started with each of your actions; it has started with each of your feelings. It has started with each of you misperceiving the other's action; it has started with each of you misperceiving the other's feelings.

WHO SHOULD STOP THE CYCLE?

If you think your partner is the only one who starts it, you probably also think that your partner needs to be the one to stop it. That means there's nothing you can do, you have no control. You might take comfort in believing that you have no responsibility, but this way of thinking also leads to feeling helpless—and staying miserable.

Perhaps, you could content yourself with self-righteous blaming. You could tell yourself that you're the innocent victim of your partner's awful wrongdoing. But you'll never be happy if this is what you think.

Instead, I'd recommend that you stop worrying about who started it, give up thinking of yourself as the innocent victim, and give up feeling self-righteous. When you do this, you get the chance to improve the most important relationship in your life. It's a good trade.

You're both involved in the cycle. The cycle is your mutual enemy. You each start it. You each keep it going. You each can change it. You each can stop it.

BUT THEIR PART IS WORSE

Your fear cycle might seem fifty-fifty. Your two parts might seem balanced and equal. That's nice in a way. You can see things in a mutual light without blaming each other. If you change your part, they are likely to change their part.

But your fear cycle might not be so even. Not all difficulties are fifty-fifty. Of course this is a matter of perception, but there also may be some truth to it. Yes, we all tend to see our partner's part as bigger. Sometimes that's blaming, but sometimes it's true.

There is a paradox here. From one perspective, both people are always involved in their fear cycles. From another perspective, one person's actions could truly be worse than the other's. I believe that there's a continuum from "all their fault" to "all your fault." It's not true that both sides are always equal.

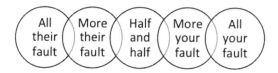

But it's hard to determine where things are on this continuum, and it's even harder to agree. Thinking about it by yourself is hard enough, but talking about it with your partner almost always degenerates into arguing and blaming.

Luckily, the question of what to do is not so uncertain. You don't need to agree where you are on this continuum to know what to do. No matter how much or little your partner contributes to the difficulty, you should still change your part. The more intense things are, the more carefully you should think about what changes you need to make. But change something. Changing your part is dramatically easier than changing theirs.

If you think things are all their fault—or all your fault—get some help. Get someone to give you another perspective. Get someone to help you figure out what to do. Here are some examples of times to get help:

- You or your partner is physically violent
- You or your partner is emotionally abusive
- You or your partner is an addict or an alcoholic
- You or your partner is having an affair
- You or your partner has serious mental health problems

For suggestions on where to get help, see Resources for Getting Professional Help.

If you think things are more your fault, you've got some work to do. Roll up your sleeves and start changing your part. As you change your part, there's a good chance that your partner will change theirs too.

If you think things are more their fault, don't just tell them they need to change. Criticizing them will not make them more receptive. Be especially careful to not use your arrow to get them to change theirs. Instead, change your own part and see what happens. See whether changing your contribution to your cycle has a positive effect on your partner. Give it some time.

↓ ↓ ↓

In this chapter you've seen how your four words combine to make your relationship's fear cycle—the worst possible combination of your deepest fears and worst reactions. If you need help condensing your fear cycle into just four words, exercise 14 might be useful.

- The less time you spend in your fear cycle, the happier you'll be.
- The more time you spend in your fear cycle, the less happy you'll be.

PART II

CHANGE YOUR FEAR CYCLE TO A LOVE CYCLE

CHAPTER FIVE

CHANGE YOUR PART OF THE CYCLE

In order to turn around and do something better, we must first escape the vicious circle of self-righteousness and denial.
—Desmond Tutu

THE POWER OF INSIGHT

Your four words have power. They help you see your fear cycle, and change it.

Sigmund Freud explained the power of insight. His psychoanalytic method involved becoming aware of previously unconscious connections in a person's life. This involved new realizations that led to better lives. As you become conscious of your fear cycle, you may have seen some new connections. You may have had some new insights.

My insight was that anger about withdrawal led to more withdrawal. My anger doesn't get me what I need; it gets me the opposite. When I really understood this, I was in new territory. This realization changed my life.

Is there some insight like that for you?

CHANGING BEHAVIOR, FEELINGS, AND THOUGHTS

Since Freud, there's been much debate about how people change. There was major debate between insight and behavior change. Behaviorists think that pursuing insight is an error. They think that behavior is the most important thing to change. Once behavior is changed, problems are solved.

By contrast, humanistic therapists feel that emotion is the road to deep and lasting change. They believe that feelings drive behavior, and therefore feelings need to change first.

Cognitive therapists believe that ideas are the most important thing to change. They believe that thought is the causative link between events and feelings. What we think about events determines how we'll feel about them. So if you want change, change your thinking.

There have been decades of debate about which is most important: insight, behavior, feelings or thought.

It's our opinion that they're all important, and all connected. If you change any one, the other three will change. Therefore, we take a practical approach and suggest you change whatever is easiest. If you look at these schools of thought on our diagram, the two arrows are behavior and the two circles are feelings.

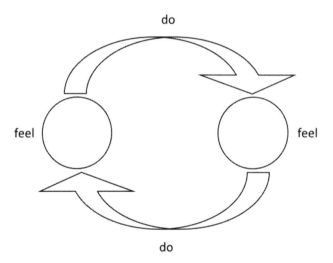

Thought is located in each of the gaps between each feeling and each behavior:

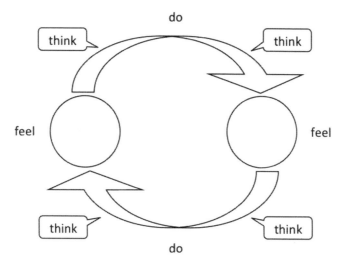

The way you think about their behavior determines how you feel. If I think Deborah is withdrawing because she doesn't want to be with me, I'll feel abandoned. But if I think Deborah is withdrawing because she's scared, I'll feel compassion. There's a world of difference between those two.

Also, the way you think about your own feelings affects how you behave. If I think my anger is justified and righteous and other people need to hear it, I'll go ahead and tell them. If I think my anger is likely to make things worse and push people further away, I'll find a way to calm down. I'll take the time to think about what I really want out of the situation and how to move toward that.

The diagram shows the relationship between doing, feeling, and thinking. The whole picture represents insight. All of these are important. Any of them can help you make things better.

A THOUGHT EXPERIMENT

Here's an experiment to consider. Think about your partner's arrow— the behavior you dislike. Suppose you wanted to see just how much of this behavior they would do. How could you create the extreme version of your partner's arrow?

The answer is: shoot the extreme version of your own arrow at them. The more you shoot your arrow, the more they shoot theirs.

For me, getting really angry would make Deborah really withdraw. In theory, I could get angry enough that she would divorce me. I'm not about to do that. That's not what I want. I don't want Deborah to leave; I'm not interested in her extreme withdrawal.

That's the point: If you don't like your partner's arrow, don't do yours.

THE SIMPLEST WAY TO END A FEAR CYCLE

We'll talk about many ways to end a fear cycle, but let's start with the simplest.

Your arrow causes theirs. So reverse this: Not shooting your arrow causes them not to shoot theirs. The simplest way to end your fear cycle is to stop shooting your arrow.

Instead, do something different at those moments. Don't tell yourself, "They made me do it." No excuses. No ifs, ands, or buts. Don't shoot your arrow—no matter what.

Your arrow is something you control. Yes, it's only one part of your cycle. Sure, there are other parts. But it's the one part you control. You can't control your feelings and thoughts, but you can control your words and actions. So, control them. Don't let your arrow be automatic and inevitable. This is the easiest part of the cycle to change. Make a decision: Just don't do it. Start right now; there's no better time.

I don't have to get angry. Deborah doesn't have to withdraw. We've done each of these many times, but we don't have to keep doing them. We can choose. We don't have to go with our first reaction. We can do something different.

DON'T SHOOT YOUR ARROW

First I decided no more bad language, name-calling, or insults. Then I decided no more yelling. Then we decided not to talk about the other's family when we were angry. Then we decided to not talk about splitting up when we were angry. All of these were good decisions.

Bit by bit I've reduced the intensity of the anger that I express to Deborah. Back in the day, that anger might reach a level of five or six on a scale of ten. These days, it's level one or two.

Deborah's glad that she met me after I was done with my level eight days. If we'd met during that period in my life, we wouldn't be together. I would have scared her too much.

I still feel intense anger occasionally, but I don't talk about it right then. I wait for the intensity to diminish. Once in a while I get angrier than I should. But, these days, I stop myself as soon as I can. I back off and calm down. I remember how I want to be. I feel regret and remorse, and I apologize. I let Deborah know I'm sorry, that I realize this is wrong and it scares her. I also renew my commitment to reducing my intensity.

The opposite would be feeling entitled to my reaction. Rather than feeling remorse, someone could feel self-righteous and justified. I hope this isn't you. I hope you don't feel that your fight or flight is warranted, or legitimate, or "just the way I am." If you defend your arrow and your right to shoot it, you won't get out of your fear cycle anytime soon.

If your partner is the one who defends his or her arrow, you have a different type of problem. We'll discuss how to handle that situation in the next chapter.

DON'T SHOOT, NO MATTER WHAT

Changing your arrow isn't easy and it's hardest when you're feeling threatened. But that's the most important time. I need to stop getting angry—especially when I feel abandoned—because that's when I get the angriest. Deborah needs to stop withdrawing—especially when she feels intimidated—because that's when she withdraws the most.

You can't say, "I won't shoot my arrow, except when I feel my circle." You have to say, "I won't shoot my arrow, especially when I feel my circle." Otherwise you'll just stay in your fear cycle. To change your arrow, you've got to stop your instinctive reaction. You'll feel the urge to react; your task is to restrain that urge.

Deborah and I have worked hard to undo our angry/withdraw cycle, and we've made a lot of progress over the years. I remember one of our earliest methods. It seems funny now, but it was very helpful at the time. In our previous home, our front door opened into a foyer. To the right was our dining room; to the left was our living room. Whenever I was angry about something, one of us would stand in the living room and the other would stand in the dining room. We had about fifteen feet and two doorways between us. That distance made Deborah feel comfortable enough to have a conversation. It gave her enough distance to stay involved.

We had to set up these conversations ahead of time; we had to both agree to talk. Mutual consent was part of the plan. This compromise met Deborah's need for safety and my need for involvement. It put limits on my anger—I couldn't get very close to her. It put limits on Deborah's withdrawal—she couldn't get very far away. Fifteen feet worked well for us at the time.

Since then, we've reduced the anger and the withdrawal substantially. We don't need the two-room method any more. My goal is to not get angry at Deborah. I don't want to express my anger in a scary, threatening way ever again. I might want to discuss a disagreement, a problem, or a change. But I don't want to do this harshly. I'd like to do this lovingly, not angrily.

Of course, I don't succeed all the time. I think I get too angry a few times a year. Deborah would say I get too angry a few times a season. Of course, she's got a much lower threshold. She might include a displeased expression on my face, or a tension in my neck muscles. I don't doubt that these things happen, and I don't doubt that I feel angry some of these times. But as long as I don't say or do anything in anger, I count that as not getting angry

Also, Deborah withdraws a lot less. When she sees me upset, she coaches herself, "Don't withdraw. Don't withdraw." She's succeeded at continuing the conversation where previously she wouldn't have. I've definitely noticed the difference. Deborah tells herself, "He just wants to be a team," as a way of reframing my concern. It's not that I'm angry at her; it's that I want more teamwork. That thought helps her stay involved. So now we can have disagreements from just a few feet apart. It's nice that there's much less anger and much less withdrawing.

How to Not Shoot Your Arrow

One way of not shooting your arrow is the action strategy. You choose a new behavior to do at those moments. Choose something very different from your arrow. Make it simple, so you can do it when you're upset.

For instance, when I'm feeling angry my new behavior is to ask for a break. Then I walk away and calm down. Asking for a break is very different from raising my voice about what I don't like. No matter what I'm feeling, no matter what I'm thinking, no matter what just happened—when I take a break I'm changing our fear cycle.

Think of something you could do. Maybe it's the opposite action of shooting your arrow. Maybe it's something that would make shooting your arrow impossible. Be sure your new plan is specific, and something you can really do. Then try it the next two or three times your cycle is beginning. This is called behavior change—intentionally choosing a new behavior that will have different results.

A second way of not shooting your arrow is the "feeling strategy." Take the time to sit with your feelings before springing into action. Like the action strategy, this method involves slowing things down—shifting from an automatic, instinctive reaction to more considered response. You'll probably be aware of anger or fear first. They're part of fight and flight. As you get in touch with your deeper feelings, you'll probably feel some kind of hurt or loneliness.

Your feelings are unique; they may be different from these. But you need to explore beyond your first emotions. Perhaps you have a combination of fear and yearning. Perhaps you fear that, "We'll never be really close," while you yearn for a truly intimate, caring connection. Perhaps you fear "I'll never be truly safe," while you yearn for a truly deep sense of security and peace. When you get in touch with your deeper feelings, you're less likely to keep the negative cycle going—and more likely to connect.

A third way to not shoot your arrow is the "thinking strategy." Before acting, think about what would be best. Use the ideas in this book. Remember your usual reaction. Think about what you've usually done in the past. Remember fight and flight. Think about your fear cycle.

Ask yourself if there might be some other explanation for your partner's behavior. Ask yourself whether your partner might be feeling vulnerable. Ask yourself whether your feeling might be an overreaction. Ask yourself what you could do instead of your arrow. Any of these thoughts may help you not react. When you can think about things in a different way, you may feel differently and act differently.

Fourth is the "insight strategy." Be aware of what's happening. See and feel your fear cycle. Remember your four words. Remember how fight and flight cause each other. When you "get" this—right in the midst of your fear cycle—you'll be seeing the big picture. You'll know that this is so different from what you want. You'll have compassion for your partner and for yourself. Any of these insights can help shift your thoughts, feelings, and actions.

You can interrupt your fear cycle by changing your actions, feelings, thinking, or your insight. When you change any one of these, the others will follow.

BECAUSE YOU LOVE THEM

The most important reason to hold back your arrow is love. You know your partner's worst feeling—of course you don't want them to feel this way. I certainly don't want Deborah to feel intimidated. I might be angry, but I don't want her to feel threatened. I'm not interested in intimidating anybody—especially not her.

Yes, I think she's oversensitive. Yes, I think she feels intimidated more than some other people do. But nobody's perfect. Sure, Deborah has some flaws and some vulnerabilities. In my opinion, this is one of them. But she's got so many wonderful qualities too.

I restrain my anger because I don't want Deborah to feel scared. I choose to limit my range of expression because of her vulnerability. This is the nature of relationships—people accommodate one another. Accommodating someone can be positive; it doesn't have to be negative. It can be caring, considerate, and kind.

You know that your arrow hits their vulnerability. You don't want them to feel that way. So don't shoot your arrow, even when you're upset. There is also a selfish reason to hold back your arrow. Shooting your arrow leads to them shooting their arrow right back at you. You don't want that. Do you see how this plays out for the two of you? Do you see how your two arrows cause each other?

THE WORST WAY TO TRY TO BREAK FREE

The worst way to try to break out of your fear cycle is to try to focus on changing your partner's behavior. Think about this one carefully, because you might be doing it. For me, this would be trying to get Deborah not to withdraw. For Deborah, it would be trying to get me not to get angry. Yes, those changes would be good. But it's an error to try to change the other person first, instead of changing ourselves first.

Like it or not, you can't force someone else to change. Restraining their fight or flight goes on inside them. You can't do it for them; they have to do it themselves. You can ask them to change, but you can't control whether they do it or not.

Even worse, we often try to change our partner's arrow by using our own arrow. This is the worst possible tool. Unfortunately, many people do this. It's a common strategy, but a very poor one. It may be what you've been doing. If so, it's time to stop. Don't do it anymore. It's time for a change. If you want to get out of a hole, stop digging.

☽ ☽ ☽

New insight, new feelings, new thoughts, and new actions change your fear cycle. You can get out of your fear cycle by understanding it. A good first step is to stop shooting your arrow.

CHAPTER SIX

THREE MORE WAYS TO CHANGE YOUR PART

Accustom yourself continually to make many acts of love, for they enkindle and melt the soul.

— Saint Teresa of Avila, *Maxims for Her Nuns*

Each of your four words shows a way to break out of your fear cycle. In the last chapter we explained how to change your arrow. In this chapter we'll talk about how to change your circle, their arrow, and their circle. If you don't change them, each of these could keep you trapped in your fear cycle. You'll stay stuck if you:

- resent his or her arrow
- ignore his or her circle
- feel victimized because of your circle
- feel self-righteous about your own arrow.

You don't want to stay locked in your fear cycle; you want to break out of it. It doesn't matter how you break out of your cycle, it matters that you do. You'll have to break out many times. Maybe one way will be best for you; maybe you'll use many different ways. Maybe you'll stop shooting your arrow. Maybe you'll use one these three other possibilities.

CHANGE YOUR CIRCLE

First let's consider the feeling in your circle. When this feeling gets too intense, you may become flooded—overwhelmed by emotion.

At those times you don't think clearly and your self-control is diminished. You're reactive and impulsive; you do things that you regret.

Another danger with your circle is blaming. You can tell yourself that you wouldn't feel this way, if you didn't have this particular partner. When you feel wounded it's tempting to see yourself as the innocent victim and your partner as the bad perpetrator. You might decide that your hurt or lonely feeling is all your partner's fault.

That's not usually true. Although your partner is triggering your vulnerability, your circle is probably a feeling you've had before. Your circle was probably an issue before you met your partner. It's probably been a lifelong vulnerability. But when you feel this hurt, you can forget your history, and just blame your partner.

LET YOURSELF FEEL YOUR EMOTION

The feeling in your circle is unpleasant, but it's here to help you. Begin by allowing yourself to feel this emotion—without trying to make it go away. Feel it, but don't act it out. Don't spring into action. Take some time for reflection, understanding, and moderation.

Don't rush to do something just to make your feeling go away. Let the feeling be. Sit with it. Emotion won't kill you. You can feel fear, hurt or loneliness and still survive. Some people call this "emotion tolerance," some call it mindfulness.

How does one feel emotion? First of all breathe; don't hold your breath. Then, notice the sensations in your body. Is there heat, tightness, tingling, or heaviness somewhere? Pay attention to your sensations. Focus on them. Imagine that the air you breathe in is going to these places, and imagine exhaling from there as well.

Notice whether your sensations shift. Do they get more intense? Or less? Do they move? Do they have colors? Do they have sounds? Do these change? Don't try to direct your sensations. If they shift, fine. If they don't shift, that's also fine.

As you do this, your attention is likely to wander—probably back to your thoughts about the situation. When you notice your mind wandering, gently bring your attention back to your sensations. Don't get angry at yourself for losing focus; just gently bring your attention back to your feelings. You'll probably have to do this many times.

As you allow yourself to explore your feeling, you may discover a range of emotions you hadn't noticed. Usually I feel angry at first— at what someone else has done. Then I realize that I feel hurt too, because I'm not getting something I need. Often there's a fear too— that this could get worse. Underneath is a feeling of loneliness and a yearning for connection. There is also despair, a sense that I'll never be truly loved, that I'm unlovable, that I'll always be alone.

This kind of exploration is unpleasant for me. I don't like having these feelings. Each is worse than the next. But when I allow these feelings—with compassion rather than self-hate—I'm doing deep self-soothing. Yes, I have these awful feelings, but I'm still here, still breathing, still surviving.

By tolerating our feelings without panicking, we allow those feelings to change. When you can tolerate despair, eventually there's a natural flow toward some kind of hope. At the worst moment in my life, when I felt the most alone, I eventually felt a deep love and acceptance. The words that came to me were, "I am still a child of God." You'll learn to have your own self-soothing—it might be similar, or it might be very different.

I also explore the feelings in my circle throughout my life history. I remember some of the times I felt most lonely and hopeless. I see these feelings in my previous marriage and in my childhood. As I trace these feelings back in my life, I'm shifting away from thinking that it's all Deborah's fault.

These are my issues. They've been with me my whole life. These are the life lessons I need to learn, the challenges I need to face. This is my work. I wish it weren't, but it is. You've got something you're working on too.

There are many different ways you could think about this. Philosophy, religion, spirituality, and psychotherapy each have ideas about the purpose of suffering. Most talk about some redeeming quality of these experiences. You may find some solace and comfort in such teachings.

Letting yourself feel your feelings is different from reacting with fight or flight. It's another way to break out of your fear cycle.

CHANGE THE WAY YOU RESPOND TO THEIR ARROW

Now let's consider their arrow. You don't like this behavior. It may be the thing you like least about your partner. When they do it, you feel bad.

There are many dangers with their arrow. The first is retaliation, the tendency to follow their bad behavior with yours. You might feel compelled to shoot your arrow back at them. You could think that it's right (and good) to shoot your arrow. You might justify retaliation.

You might think, "They hurt me, so I'm going to hurt them," or, "I'll show them how it feels." We all have thoughts like this, but the way out of your cycle is to not put these impulses into action. If you feel like striking back, it's time to take a break and calm down. Anything else is guaranteed trouble.

Retaliation definitely escalates fear cycles. Some of the worst moments are times of retaliation. When both people do things to hurt the other—because they've been hurt themselves—real damage can be done. Words are said that are hard to forget; actions are taken that are hard to undo. Retaliation can change the course of your life in a very bad way.

I'd suggest you not give yourself permission to retaliate—no matter what. Vengeance and revenge don't lead to a good place. When you're feeling your circle, it's an especially bad time to retaliate.

Another danger with their arrow is disgust. You could feel disgusted that they allow themselves to do this. You might think, "I would never do that." You might think that no one should treat another person this way. But you have to be careful about feeling contempt for your partner and coming across judgmental, condescending, or superior.

A final danger is feeling intolerance toward his or her arrow. You might say to yourself, "I can't live with this." You could take this behavior as proof that you two are incompatible. You could define this as an irreconcilable difference. You could decide it's the reason you need to end the relationship.

With certain severe problems, this might be your wisest course of action. If your partner won't stop their abuse, their affair, or their addiction, it might indeed be best for you to end the relationship. But with more moderate problems, breaking up might not be the only way to solve the problem. Yes, you need your partner to stop shooting their arrow, but not all arrows are hopeless deal breakers.

DO SOMETHING DIFFERENT

Your partner's arrow can be a way out of your fear cycle—if you respond differently when they shoot it.

When Deborah withdraws, I feel angry, and my impulse is to confront her. But I don't want to do that because it would worsen our fear cycle. I have two new responses. One is to ask, "Do you need some time to think about this?" Usually Deborah says yes, and we agree to talk later. She thinks it was obvious that she just needed some time to think, but it wasn't obvious to me. I wasn't sure she wanted to think about it or talk about it—at all. I'm glad to know she's thinking, and I'm glad when we've made a time to talk.

My other new response is to do nothing. I let her withdraw without calling attention to it. I don't make a big deal of her withdrawal. I just act as if she had called time-out. Her pulling back tells me she needs to take a break. My doing nothing tells her that's okay with me. I'd prefer to do this in words, but that's not Deborah's style. I'm the talker, she's not. So just like I go along with her need to take a break, I go along with her nonverbal way of saying it.

Maybe the problem is something small that I don't need to worry about, or maybe it's something big that I do need to discuss. If so, I make a mental note. Sometimes I write it down. But I don't say any of this to Deborah right then.

That's new for me. My old way would be to angrily confront her withdrawal. My new way is to stay calm and keep quiet. That's a big difference. I'm not contributing to our fear cycle; I'm not making things worse.

You might think about a new and different response to your partner's arrow. Choose one that would be the opposite of shooting your own arrow.

CHANGE YOUR THINKING

You also want to think differently about their arrow. You want to reframe it. When you put a new frame around a picture it can look very different. Try a sympathetic frame. Their arrow is fight or flight. They're doing it because they feel threatened. Think about that threatened feeling.

I know that Deborah withdraws because she's fearful. So I think, "She must be scared," rather than "She's abandoning me." Both are true, but the new frame helps me focus on how bad she must feel— rather than the bad thing she's doing to me.

Deborah does the same. She knows I get angry because I feel left alone, so when I'm angry she tries to see how I might be feeling abandoned. It's a lot easier to deal with an abandoned person than an angry one. We both look for the circle behind the arrow.

There's a saying, "Be kind. Everyone you meet is fighting a great battle." That's this same reframe. Underneath your partner's arrow is their great battle. When we focus on their distress, we naturally change how we react.

The quickest way to do this is to memorize, "They're _____, so they must be feeling _____." In the first blank you put their arrow; in the second blank you put their circle. Our reframing is:

- Deborah's withdrawing, so she must be feeling intimidated.
- David's angry, so he must be feeling abandoned.

There are many possible ways to reframe something. The helpful ones are positive attitudes rather than negative ones. They give your partner the benefit of the doubt. Instead of thinking "Deborah's withdrawal is so cold," I could think "She wants us to calm down." Instead of thinking, "Deborah is too fearful," I could think, "She's right, this conversation could escalate."

Instead of thinking, "David's anger is bad," Deborah could think, "He's got some point he's trying to make." Instead of thinking, "David's anger is the cause of our problems," Deborah could think that we do the anger/withdrawal cycle together.

Pick a positive reframing you can use when your fear cycle starts. Challenge your old ways of thinking. Think about your four words in a new way—a way that leads out of your fear cycle. Don't think about those words in the old way—the way that leads right back into your fear cycle.

The emotional difference is like night and day. Reframing shifts you from feeling threatened, to feeling compassion for the hard battle your partner is fighting. When you do this, your partner will sense the difference, and your fear cycle will change.

REMEMBER THEIR CIRCLE

Now let's consider your partner's circle. One danger here is if you don't know your partner's feelings. Perhaps they haven't told you about these feelings; or perhaps you haven't listened when they did. It's easy to see how this could happen. When a fear cycle is spinning, we all pay attention to threats, not underlying feelings. Usually, underlying feelings the part of a fear cycle we know least well.

A worse danger is if you don't want to know your partner's feelings. Maybe you're so angry you just want them to stop behaving badly. Maybe you think, "Who cares about how they feel!" Maybe you just don't want to be criticized or blamed any more. All these thoughts are understandable, but unfortunately they can come across as not caring.

Another danger is assuming the worst about your partner's intentions. You could assume that they want to hurt you and make you feel bad. You could assume they like being cruel, malicious, or vengeful.

When you assume the worst about their intentions, you get judgmental and self-righteous. When you decide that your partner is bad, you blame her or him, and your compassion leaves. You also assume there's nothing you can do. These assumptions make things much worse.

My worst assumption would be that Deborah really doesn't care about me. I could decide that's why she withdraws at moments of intensity—because she doesn't care if I'm troubled or hurting. If she did care, she couldn't possibly leave me alone in these situations. All she cares about is herself. She doesn't really want to be with me.

Thank goodness I don't actually believe any of this. Thank goodness none of this is actually true. But at some of our worst moments—when I've been really upset and she's pulled back—these thoughts have gone through my mind.

Those were bad moments. I recall disagreements about some family matters where I really felt I was on my own. It seemed like I wasn't going to get any help from Deborah. It felt like she didn't care. I truly felt alone.

That feeling of mine was a direct result of my worst assumption. When I make a better assumption, things feel more hopeful. When I assume that Deborah feels scared or hurt, I realize she's pulling back out of fear. She doesn't want to leave me alone, she's just scared. My better assumption evokes my compassion, not my resentment.

She's fighting a great battle. That's what helps me get back to being kind.

HAVE COMPASSION

Your partner's circle gives you the opportunity to feel compassion. The reason they're fighting or flying is that they're fearful. If you can focus on their underlying fear, you can change your cycle. Take your eyes off their arrow and look at the circle behind it. Focus on the vulnerable feeling that's driving their behavior. They're feeling threatened; have compassion for that.

I know that Deborah withdraws when she's feeling intimidated, so my goal is to focus on that feeling. When Deborah seems withdrawn or distant, I've started asking her, "What's going on with you, sweetie?" "What's happening?" "Are you troubled about something?" This is very different from angrily demanding, "Stop withdrawing!"

Deborah does the same for me. When she sees me angry, she considers if I might be feeling abandoned in some way. She asks me about that. Instead of saying, "Don't get angry!" she says, "What's wrong, honey?" She wants to address the feelings underneath my anger.

Compassion is deciding to focus on your partner's feelings (their circle). It means not focusing on what they're doing wrong (their arrow), what they're accusing you of doing wrong (your arrow), or on how badly you feel (your circle). Although this is hard to do, it works amazingly well. When you wholeheartedly have compassion for their feelings, you're no longer a threat. You're someone who cares, someone who loves them. They'll be less reactive, and your fear cycle will go away.

Of course this works in the other direction as well. Life is certainly easier when your partner does this for you too. But don't wait for them to go first. It's so much easier to change yourself than it is to change your partner. It's better to go first yourself. Give it a try. Don't demand mutuality at first.

☆ ☆ ☆

In the previous chapter we talked about breaking out of your fear cycle by not shooting your arrow. In this chapter we've looked at the three other places to break out of your fear cycle: your circle, their arrow, and their circle.

- Soothe your own feelings (your circle)
- Reframe their behavior (their arrow)
- Have compassion for their feelings (their circle)

CHAPTER SEVEN

UNDERSTANDING CHILDHOOD INFLUENCES

Those who can't remember the past are condemned to repeat it.

—George Santayana, *Reasons in Common Sense*

THE HISTORY BEHIND HURT FEELINGS

Your hurt feeling, whatever word you chose for it, is probably connected to your previous experience. You may have felt this way in previous relationships; you may have known this feeling as a child.

That's true for Deborah. She's always been very uncomfortable around someone who was angry. It's always made her feel very frightened. Her father was a problem drinker. Sometimes when angry, he was violent with Deborah's mother. So of course Deborah was deeply afraid—she was a little girl with a big, angry father.

On occasion, Deborah's mother could also be angry and violent. When her mother was in extreme distress, she would threaten to harm Deborah—a little girl who unfortunately also had a scary, angry mother. Deborah is still vigilant to this day. She still "sleeps with one eye open" and doesn't like to be surprised. Anger is very scary to her, it sets off her alarms.

I know why she's frightened and why her fear is so intense. If I were to say, "I'm not so angry" or "What's the big deal?" or "What are you so worried about?" that would be pretty thoughtless.

Meanwhile, I have to admit that I have been pretty enraged at times. In the last two decades I've tried hard to change that, but there was a time when I raised my voice a lot. I don't yell anymore, but I do still feel anger—sometimes intensely—and Deborah can still see

81

it in my face, even if I'm not actively expressing it. My anger is much milder now, but it can still seem scary and hurtful. Deborah thinks to herself: If someone cherished me, they wouldn't scare me like this. I certainly don't want to hurt Deborah, or scare her. But when I get intense, that's what happens. I just want to talk about something, but she feels scared and hurt.

One example is our standing disagreement about how intensely to exercise. I think "Push hard," Deborah thinks, "Don't push too hard." That's not so awful. It's a legitimate difference of opinion. No big deal. People are entitled to different opinions. Except that's not how it plays out.

I'm a cyclist, and part of cycling is pushing myself. Pushing is the key to getting in shape, developing fitness, and increasing speed and endurance. Each year I push myself to get back in shape after the off-season. But Deborah sees how exhausted I look, and how tired I can be, and sometimes how grumpy. And she also worries about crashes and injuries and muscle strains—all of which have happened. These are all valid concerns. But the problem happens when I get angry, or when Deborah thinks I'm angry. Many times she's raised the issue, "Honey, I think you need to take it easier," and she can see the anger on my face. Sometimes I've argued with her; sometimes I gotten mad at her for holding me back.

I've come to call this disagreement "resistance training" because I have to train in spite of Deborah's resistance. She says, "Don't leave so early," "Don't come back so late," "Don't ride so long," "Don't ride so hard," "Why do you have to push yourself?" From her point of view, she's damned if she does and damned if she doesn't. If she talks to me, I'm going to get angry. If she doesn't talk to me, I'm going to train too hard and get grumpy.

Deborah knows that I feel angry about her resistance. Even when I don't say it, she can see the way I breathe, my body movements, and my facial expressions. I'm not grimacing or sighing or clenching my teeth—it's much subtler. Although I think I'm staying calm, she can see the irritation that I feel. I don't like that she's afraid of me. On so many levels, I would never hurt her. But I need to see that my very natural reactions of irritation—even small, unexpressed ones—scare her. Until I see that, things don't make sense.

If you're the fighter, there's something like that going on for you, too. You need to understand your partner's fear when you fight. You need to put yourself in their shoes.

The History behind Lonely Feelings

Loneliness is my greatest fear and deepest vulnerability—especially when I'm upset and I want someone to comfort me. I can clearly see this pattern throughout my life, in so many major crises.

It was clear when my ex-wife left me many years ago. I was devastated. I was sure we would be together forever. I was so shocked when she said she was leaving. I had no idea that things were that bad. We were planning a life together; we had a child together; we had a business together. I begged her to talk to me and tell me what was so wrong. I asked her what she wanted me to change. No luck. She was in full flight mode, and the more intensely I urged her to talk, the more she needed to get away.

I felt so abandoned that I wasn't even sure I wanted to go on living. It seemed like everything in my life was ending— my family, my work, my place in our community, my whole definition of who I was. For seven years I had been David-and-Annie. That was my name. That was how I was known. Now that was all changing. It seemed that my life was over.

Indeed, the life I had known was truly over. I gave up my business. I went back to graduate school. I changed careers. I learned how to be a single parent. Some years later, I learned how to endure periods of time without my son. That divorce was the biggest abandonment in my adult life.

But my feelings of abandonment go even further back—all the way back to my infancy. In most ways I wasn't abandoned at all. I had a stable household with two caring parents who were very interested in my well-being. I never went without. I had every advantage. But there was one way in which I did feel abandoned. As a baby, I had celiac disease and was often pretty uncomfortable. I cried a lot. There were a lot of times when I wanted to be held and comforted, but was left to cry alone.

My parents took care of me so well in so many ways, but they weren't there to hold me when I was hurting. Maybe no parent could have been there enough. A child with Celiac disease can be overwhelming for anyone. But nonetheless, I felt hurt and abandoned. That was my first experience of loneliness.

That feeling gets stirred up when Deborah withdraws. That's why abandonment runs so deep for me. I'm especially sensitive to feeling lonely and alone—just the way Deborah is especially sensitive to fear and anger.

UNDERSTANDING YOUR BACKGROUND

Do the components of your fear cycle replay some part of your childhood like ours do? Have you been treated this way before? Felt this way before? Reacted this way before? Did something like this happen to someone else in your family? If so, this similarity could explain why your fear cycle is so intense.

Or perhaps your fear cycle is the opposite of your childhood. Maybe no one ever treated you this way, you never felt like this, and you never reacted this way before. Maybe it's not similarity, maybe it's difference that explains why your fear cycle is so uncomfortable.

At the bottom of the diagram we add two houses to represent childhood. In these houses, we put phrases that connect the fear cycle to each person's past.

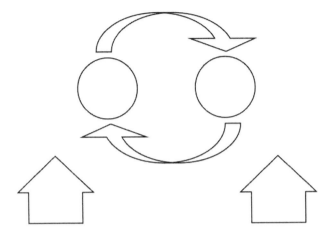

Here are some questions to help to choose these phrases.

Is this a Reminder of What Happened Before?

First, consider your partner's arrow. Did someone act like this when you were growing up? Deborah withdraws. I ask myself, "Did someone withdraw from me in my childhood?" The answer is yes. Both my parents did. They were very nice people, and wonderful parents in many ways. They provided so much for me. But they were emotionally distant. My father was detached and intellectual; my mother was not very physically affectionate.

I remember them taking very good care of me. When I was sick or injured, they were right there. My father was a physician, and my mother was very involved in the world of medicine. I got great physical care, but not such great emotional support.

I don't remember being emotionally comforted. I don't remember being held and feeling better. I didn't know that touch could be soothing. The emotional distance was tough for me. Wouldn't you know it, that's the issue I have with Deborah too. Once again the person

I'm closest to tends to pull back emotionally. Does your partner's arrow resemble the way someone treated you?

Second, consider your circle—your hurt or lonely feeling. Did you feel like that as a child? Some people experienced the same treatment, so of course they have the same emotional reactions. Other people experienced different treatment, but still had the same emotions. Feeling abandoned, for instance, could come from emotional withdrawal, or it could come from actually being left.

I feel abandoned when Deborah and I are in our fear cycle. I felt abandoned as a child too. I had to take care of myself emotionally. I was on my own with my feelings. If I wanted to be soothed, I had to soothe myself. That gets replayed today, word for word. Think about whether the emotions in your circle may be similar to the way you felt as a child.

Third, consider your arrow—your fight or flight. Did you react now the same way you reacted as a child? I ask myself: Did I get angry as a child? Yes I did. I threw tantrums. I cried and screamed. When I felt hurt and lonely, I got angry.

- For me: Both parents withdrew emotionally. I felt abandoned. I got angry.
- For Deborah: Both parents got angry. She felt intimidated. She withdrew.

It might be the same for you, or it might not. Everybody is different. Maybe your replay is with just one parent. Maybe you're replaying something with a sibling, a grandparent, or some other significant caretaker. If you need help with this, exercise 15 leads you through these questions.

If you find a similarity to your past, you've discovered something important. But this similarity does not mean that you're to blame. It does not mean that this fear cycle is all your fault. Your partner's childhood contributes to your cycle as well.

ARE YOU RELIVING SOMEONE ELSE'S EXPERIENCE?

Some people don't find similarities between their cycle and their childhood. This might be because you're not replaying your experience. Maybe you're replaying someone else's. Maybe something like this happened to another person in your family. Maybe you noticed, sympathized, and empathized. Maybe you felt bad about it, and felt bad for them. You may have decided that this would never happen to you. You may have done things to make sure that it didn't. You may have also decided you'd never put yourself in this position.

For instance, my mother felt lonely when my father was away during World War II. After the war, he was spent long hours at the hospital. Many evenings at home he read journals, wrote papers, and prepared presentations. She knew these things were important, but she still felt lonely.

My father felt lonely too. He was too busy—he had too much work and not enough time. My loneliness is like his. I can be too busy. I can make too much time for work and not enough time for friends and family. Like my father, when I'm lonely I work harder—then feel empty, work to fill the emptiness, still feel empty, and work harder. It's a never ending, self-defeating cycle.

So when I think about our fear cycle, I realize that my loneliness is not all Deborah's fault. Her withdrawing might trigger my loneliness, but this is a feeling I've struggled with my whole life. I felt this way before, and my father did too. He also had the drama of work and solitude. He also felt people withdraw from him. When he felt lonely he also got busy and drove people away. It's a sad legacy.

Maybe you didn't feel this way before, but one of your family members did. The roots of your fear cycle may be someone else's experience—not yours. Amazingly, it can still affect you. You loved that person; you cared about them. When something hurt that person it really affected you. Maybe you decided:

- " When I grow up I'll never let anyone treat me like that."
- "When I grow up, I'm never going to be like that."
- "When I grow up, I'm never going to treat anyone like that."

These decisions can be a lasting source of guidance and direction. They clarify who you are and who you're not, what you want and what you don't. But these decisions can also contribute to your fear cycle. They can account for the intensity of your reactions. Deborah wasn't attacked by her father—but her mother was—and Deborah witnessed it. Deborah felt the same fear of being attacked.

Maybe you didn't get angry as a child, but your mother did. Maybe now you find yourself doing it, although you swore you'd never be this way. Maybe you decided that no one would ever treat you disrespectfully the way you saw your father treat your mother. He didn't treat you that way, thank goodness, but it was awful the way he treated your mother. You swore no one would ever do that to you. You wouldn't put up with it. Maybe now, lo and behold, it's happening to you. You're not reliving your own experience; you're reliving your mother's experience.

This is unpleasant of course. No one wants this. But it's not so uncommon. Perhaps it's your time to face the same challenges that your mother faced. Maybe a grandparent dealt with the same issue; maybe a great-grandparent too. Problems can be passed from generation to generation.

The biggest replay for Deborah is her mother's ostracism. Deborah's mother struggled with many challenges. She had a difficult childhood and chronic, disabling health problems. After her broken marriage she was left with a young daughter and very little money. Without a stable home, she moved frequently and felt like an outsider in each new community, job, church and school. With thrift store clothes remade at home, she never felt like she looked acceptable. A very attractive woman, she received a lot of problematic attention from men. She felt ostracized and "less than"—again and again. She was vulnerable in a very tough world.

Deep down, Deborah still has fears about this. In spite of our many neighbors, colleagues, and friends, she can still feel left out and not good enough. She can easily feel hurt, shamed, and put down. She can withdraw very quickly. She doesn't fight, she pulls back. In this way Deborah is reliving her mother's experience. Like her mother, she struggles with the challenges of handling put-downs and rejection, and how to deal with the voices inside her own head that tell her she's inadequate. Like her mother, she hides this from the outside world. Deborah is very attractive, well-educated and successful. Most people have no idea that Deborah's life was so difficult. It's hard to believe that this confident, competent woman still has fears like this.

Deborah has handled these challenges much more successfully than her mother did. She's made a stable home and a stable marriage. She's financially secure. She is a valued member of our communities at home, at synagogue and at work. Yet her childhood insecurity still lurks underneath, and that's part of what drives our fear cycle. Underneath Deborah's feeling of intimidation lays a terror—her mother's terror—that something really dreadful could happen.

ARE YOU DEALING WITH A COMPLETELY UNFAMILIAR EXPERIENCE?

Some people don't see any resemblance between their fear cycle and their childhood. Instead, they see how different their fear cycle is from their past. That might be true for you; your early experiences may have been very different from what's going on now.

Let's ask some different questions about your childhood: First, is the way you're being treated now the opposite of the way you were treated as a child? If so, no wonder you don't like the treatment you're getting. You've had other, better connections for a long time. It's what you've come to expect. What's going on now is not the way life is supposed to be.

Second, are your feelings the opposite of the way you felt as a child? If so, no wonder you don't like these feelings. Life isn't supposed to feel like this. Of course you protest against these feelings.

The third question is whether the way you react now is the opposite of the way you reacted as a child. If I'd always been a happy kid—peaceful easy-going, loving, and kind—that would be the opposite of how I react in our fear cycle.

Something like that might be true of you. You may be reacting in a way that is totally uncharacteristic—the opposite of your usual behavior. It might be something you've never done before. It might be the opposite of the way you've always been.

If one or more elements of your fear cycle are the opposite of your childhood, try to put that into words. Perhaps you would say:

- "My parents never got angry."
- "I always felt secure."
- "I never withdrew."

Or:

- "My parents were always there for me."
- "I never felt abandoned."
- "I never got angry."

This is very important information. It explains why these things are so uncomfortable for you, and why you react so strongly. It explains why you're not used to these things and not good at handling them. Perhaps you were sheltered from some of life's difficulties until now. If this is difficult to see, exercise 16 guides you through these questions.

Is Your Relationship Bad Luck or Good?

If your fear cycle is the opposite of your childhood, you've got a big decision to make. You have to decide whether to think of your relationship as a bad luck or good.

- Bad luck: you're with someone who's wrong for you,
- Good luck: you're with someone who's teaching you something you need to learn.

Bad luck thinking goes: "This is new to me, so it must be their fault. They bring this problem our relationship, not me. It's not part of my family history. It's all them, 100 percent. I didn't realize they were this way. If I had, I wouldn't have gotten involved. Being involved with them is bad luck. "

As you can imagine, your partner won't like to hear this, and I wouldn't recommend saying it to them. Instead, you've got a serious decision to make. Maybe you don't want to be in this relationship any more. Maybe you have to decide whether to end your partnership— and when and how. These aren't easy questions. Breaking up can be hard to do.

The alternative is seeing your relationship as good luck. Good luck thinking goes: "I wonder what they're doing in my life. It sure seems uncomfortable. Maybe they're here to teach me something. Maybe there's something I need to learn. Maybe they're giving me an opportunity to become a more compassionate, well-rounded human being."

One example could sound like, "I have trouble with anger because I've never been around it. I certainly don't want to be abused, but maybe there is a moderate, reasonable type of anger that I need to learn. Maybe this is important for me." Or, "I have trouble with abandonment because I've never experienced it before. I certainly don't want to be left alone, but maybe I need to learn about a more moderate type of separation. Maybe this is an important lesson for me."

There's no way to prove whether your relationship is good luck or bad. Instead, you choose which of these to believe. Your choice makes a big difference.

How Understanding Your Childhood Helps

If you're replaying your childhood, you know which parts of your cycle are especially difficult for you. If you've received this treatment before, can you see how you're extra sensitive to it? You react to this behavior pretty strongly. Can you believe that there are people who are less sensitive—and able to tolerate more of this behavior than you can?

If you've felt this way before, your vulnerability is not all your partner's doing. Yes, your partner sets it off, but your intensity is because your feelings echo your past. These feelings have been difficult for you for a long time.

If you've reacted this way before, you may have to break a long-standing habit. No doubt this reaction served you well at some point in your life. It probably was the best option you had; it probably saved you from greater trouble. But, today you need to find another option.

Maybe someone else in your family got this treatment, or had these reactions. Maybe you're doing what they used to do. Or maybe you're doing what you wish they had done.

Whatever the origin of your reactions, beware of thinking, "That's just the way I am" and deciding that you're not going to change. If you don't change your reactions, you'll never get out of your fear cycle, and you'll never be happy.

If you think you can't change, you're right. If you think you can change, you're right. Either way it's a self-fulfilling prophecy. The way you choose to think determines your future.

WHAT IMPERFECT RELATIONSHIPS CAN TEACH YOU

If nothing like this has ever happened to you before, let's think about what your partner may be here to teach you. It might be: their arrow isn't as awful as you think. Just because you're unfamiliar with it doesn't make it bad. Maybe it's a part of life that you need to get to know. Your partner can get angry and you'll still survive. They can withdraw and you'll still be okay.

Maybe they can teach you how to handle some new feelings. Maybe you were shielded from these feelings when you were younger, but maybe that sheltered time should be over. Maybe it's time for you to experience these difficult emotions. This can be humbling, but it can also make you more compassionate.

Maybe it's good that your partner brings out new things in you. Maybe you never got angry before. Maybe you never took a firm stance. Maybe you never cried before. Maybe you never expressed your needs. Any of these might be good.

HOW YOUR PARTNER'S CHILDHOOD AFFECTS YOUR CYCLE

It's also important to know how your partner's childhood effects your fear cycle. There are a few cautions to bear in mind.

First, remember that you're just guessing. Your partner is the authority on their life and their feelings. Don't insist you know better than they do.

Second, be careful not to blame. Blaming would go like this: You identify some part of your partner's childhood that resembles your fear cycle. You conclude that your fear cycle is their fault, since they had these issues before you met them. You decide that you are an innocent victim of your partner's bad childhood and dysfunctional personality. Don't do this.

Instead:

- Use insights about yourself to get you to change.
- Use insights about your partner to develop compassion for them—not to get them to change.

With these considerations in mind, try to put yourself in your partner's shoes, and ask yourself:

- When they were a child, did someone treat them the way you do now (your arrow)?
- Did they feel the same way they do now (their circle)?
- Did they react the same way they do now (their arrow)?

If you need help with this, exercise 17 will guide you through these questions.

If, in the past, someone treated your partner the same way you do, your partner will be very sensitive to your arrow. They won't tolerate much of it. When you're not doing it, they'll imagine you are. When you are doing it, they'll exaggerate the intensity and make it more awful than it is. If they're repeating an old feeling, they'll overreact. Their emotional response will be greater than seems reasonable.

If their current reaction is the way they reacted as a child, it's going to be hard for them to change. It was probably a survival mechanism as a child. It must have served them well at some point.

If you're not seeing any ways in which your fear cycle resembles your partner's childhood—maybe your fear cycle is the opposite of your partner's childhood.

- Is your behavior the opposite of the way they were treated as a child?
- Are their feelings the opposite of how they felt as a child?
- Is their reaction the opposite of the way they reacted as a child?

Similar principles apply. If they've never been treated this way before, they'll probably be very uneasy with your arrow. They'll think it's wrong or inappropriate. They may think that no one should be treated the way you treat them. They're not good at handling this behavior of yours, because they're so unfamiliar with it.

If they've never felt this way before, these feelings probably make them very uncomfortable. They probably think that something is terribly wrong. They're not good at soothing themselves when they feel this way; they don't have a lot of practice at it.

If they've never reacted this way before, they're not going to be very good at their new reaction. They're not smooth; their behavior is awkward and overdone. If you need help, exercise 18 will guide you through considering the possibility that your cycle is the opposite of their childhood.

HOW UNDERSTANDING YOUR PARTNER'S CHILDHOOD HELPS

Understanding your partner's childhood increases your compassion for them. For Deborah, our fear cycle is a replay. When I get angry, I remind Deborah of her father. My anger isn't anywhere near as intense as his was, but I can picture what she's experiencing. I have a mental image of a scared little girl facing a big, drunk, angry man. I see him towering over her. I see her being very quiet and trying as hard as she can to not make anything worse.

When I call this picture to mind I feel compassion for that little girl. I imagine her terror. I'm sorry this ever happened to her. I don't want to scare her like that. I don't want to intimidate her. I don't want to make her feel the way she did as a child. That's the last thing I want.

Sure, at those moments, there's something I need to say. But that can wait. Sure I'm angry about something. But that doesn't mean I want to scare her. When I picture that little girl, I want to protect her, so I become kinder. By remembering her childhood, I change my anger to compassion.

I can do the same thing when Deborah withdraws. I can remind myself that withdrawing is what she learned to do when she was scared. That fits with the little girl in my picture. When I remind myself of this, I do a better job at not taking her withdrawal so personally. Yes, she's leaving me alone, but no, that's not her motive. I think to myself, "She's withdrawing because she's terrified, like she was with her father."

Calling to mind my image of a little girl with a big angry man helps me think differently about my anger, her fear, and her withdrawal. I care for that little girl. I want to protect her. This, of course, is just what Deborah needs.

A similar pattern might be true for you. Can you come up with a mental image of your partner as a child that would help? If so, try imagining that when your fear cycle is starting.

If your partner's childhood was the opposite of your fear cycle, you use that knowledge in a different way. Remind yourself, "This is hard for them because it's so new." If they've never had to deal with your behavior before, of course they're not good at it. They have no practice, they have no skills.

If they're having feelings they've never had before, of course they're uncomfortable with them. Maybe they're scared of these feelings. Maybe they imagine these feelings are intolerable.

If your partner's reaction is a totally new behavior for them, of course they're not smooth at it. They're awkward; they may overdo it or underdo it.

ADDING CHILDHOOD TO THE DIAGRAM

Here is our diagram with houses on the bottom representing our childhoods. These houses explain why we're so sensitive to the feelings and reactions in our cycle.

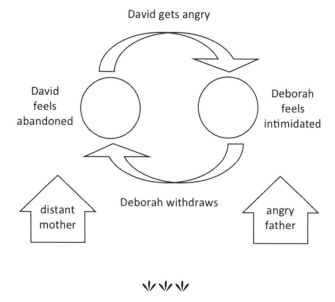

In this chapter you've considered each of your childhoods and how they affect your fear cycle. You've thought about whether your fear cycle may be replaying your past. If your childhood was the opposite of your fear cycle, you've considered whether your lack of exposure explains why these things are so difficult for you.

- Your childhoods explain why your fear cycle is so intense for each of you.
- Remembering these sensitivities helps you stay calmer, and more compassionate.

So far you've learned to understand your fear cycle. In the next chapter, we'll talk about a cycle you'll like much better—your love cycle.

CHAPTER EIGHT

YOUR LOVE CYCLE

The most important thing in life is to learn how to give out love, and to let it come in.

—Morrie Schwartz, *Tuesdays with Morrie*

Luckily, you two also have a love cycle. It's the opposite of your fear cycle. It goes round and round too; but your love cycle makes you feel good, not bad. Until this point, we've focused on problems. We looked at your fight and flight, your hurt and loneliness, and the childhood difficulties that contribute to these.

Now let's think about what you want instead. You want to feel secure, not vulnerable. You want to be kind, not reactive. You want the good parts of your childhood repeated, not the bad parts.

YOUR DREAM

Look at your fear cycle and consider the word in your circle. What would be the opposite of that feeling? That answer may be your dream.

The word in my circle is abandoned. To me, the opposite is loved— and that's my dream. That's what I really want. When I feel loved, I relax. I don't get angry. I don't drive people away.

You may think of a number of feelings that are the opposite of your greatest fear. As you think about those different feelings, see if one is the deepest, or most important, or most all-encompassing. That's the one to use.

Another way to find the best word for your dream is to consider the opposite of each of the four words in your fear cycle. Here are the words we use:

Fear cycle	Opposite
withdrawn	involved
abandoned	loved
angry	kind
intimidated	cherished

You'll have your own list. Think about which of your four opposites is most important to you. May that's your dream. Or, perhaps there's one word that captures the opposite of all four. If you need help with this, exercise 19 can guide you through the process.

When I think about our four opposites, I get the same result. The most important to me is still loved. Feeling loved might be your dream too. But there are many other dreams as well. Some people dream of safety or peace. Some dream of passion or adventure.

Think about your childhood. Is there a word for the dream that you had as a child? Maybe it was something you had then and want again. Maybe it's something you never had but always needed. Dreams are usually rooted deeply in our past.

Dr. Harville Hendrix is of the opinion that we seek our childhood dreams in our adult romantic relationships. Earlier we wanted these feelings with our parents. Now we want them with our partners.

For many of us, getting what we need—love or safety or passion—isn't so easy. It wasn't easy before, and it isn't easy now. That's the drama underlying our fear cycles. Each person's unmet needs from childhood are being replayed in today's struggle. The goal is for both of you to finally get what you truly need. It's not impossible. But to do it, you have to shift your fear cycle to a love cycle.

If you don't have your dream now, you probably have strong feelings about that. There is one helpful feeling, and one not-so-helpful feeling. They are yearning and resentment—and they're opposites.

Yearning for your dream can lead you to desire, hope, direction, and motivation. Resenting that you don't have your dream can lead you to anger, bitterness, discouragement and resignation. Resentment plunges you back into your fear cycle; yearning moves you toward your love cycle.

How Knowing Your Dream Helps

Yearning for your dream is the best reason to not do fight or flight. If I'm yearning to feel loved, I shouldn't get angry. Because when I do, people usually pull back. I end up more alone, more abandoned, and less loved.

Dr. Barry Klein taught me to ask myself three questions when I'm angry:

1. What do I really want out of this situation?
2. What's the worst thing I could do?
3. What am I going to do?

Usually, my answers are:

1. I want to be loved.
2. The worst thing I could do is get angry.
3. I am going to calm down so that I can consider my options and be more reasonable.

I want to:

- Do things that lead to feeling loved
- Not do things that lead to feeling abandoned

Try applying those ideas to yourself. Use the words for your dream and your fear. See if they make sense.

- Do things that lead to _____(your dream)
- Don't do things that lead to _____(your fear)

If you need help, exercise 21 will guide you through this process.

To move toward their dreams some people need to be more assertive, others need to be less. Deborah needs to be more assertive; I need to be less. I ask myself, "Would I give up expressing intense anger so that I could feel more loved?" Yes. Absolutely, I would. There's a question like this for you too. Would you give up your reactivity so you can have your dream? I hope you would. I think it's worth it.

The arrow in your fear cycle keeps you from your dream because it makes your partner feel bad. You need a love arrow instead—something that makes your partner feel good. If I really want to be loved, the best thing I can do is be kind and make Deborah feel cherished. When she's feeling cherished, she's naturally loving, caring, and nurturing. Something like that is true for you too.

YOUR PARTNER'S DREAM

Your partner's dream is also the opposite of your fear cycle. It may be the opposite of their childhood, or it may be something they had as a child and want again.

Deborah's dream is to feel cherished. That's the opposite of feeling intimidated. If you cherish someone, you treat them lovingly; you take good care of them. You protect them from harm; you never intimidate them. Deborah didn't feel cherished when her father and mother were angry and violent.

What's your partner's dream? May it's a word they use frequently; maybe it's a word they've never used before. If you need help finding that word, exercise 20 can help.

Remember that you're only guessing about their dream. They're the one who knows. I had guessed that Deborah's dream was "safe." I wasn't wrong, but I didn't have the best word for it. "Cherished" is a better word, with much richer, deeper meaning for her.

It's good to guess your partner's dream. Just remember that someday, when the two of you talk about it, you may revise your guess.

HOW THEIR DREAM HELPS

It's hard to remember your partner's dream when you're in your fear cycle because reactivity and fear grab your attention instead. But other times, remembering his or her dream is much easier. Use those times to think about the things you can do to support that dream. Do these things whenever you can.

From time to time I tell Deborah that I want to take care of her and treat her special. It's good for me to say this out loud. She also feels cherished when I brush her hair. She feels cherished when I call her "sweetie" or tell her how much I appreciate what she does. She even feels cherished when I take care of our bookkeeping. The more I make her feel cherished at easy times, the better things go at difficult times. The more she feels cherished, the more our fear cycle softens.

You'll benefit from nurturing your partner's dream whenever you can. Find small things that you can do often. The more your partner feels like this, the better things will be.

PUTTING YOUR DREAMS ON THE DIAGRAM

At the top of the diagram are two hearts for your dreams. These hearts represent what you yearn for in the future.

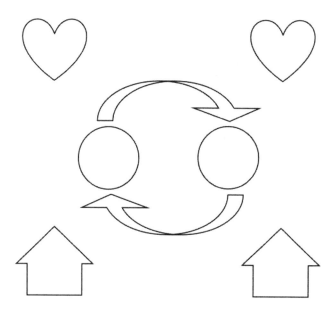

Our complete diagram looks like this:

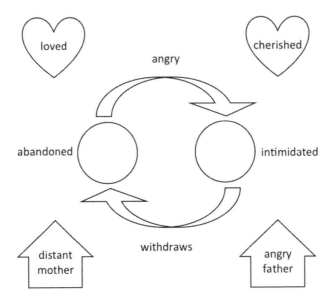

We like to use as few words as possible; you might want to do the same. That way it's easier to remember.

The Cycle You Prefer

Just as every couple has a fear cycle, so every couple has a love cycle. Your fear cycle is made of your hurt feelings and defensive reactions. Your love cycle is made of your good feelings and loving actions. Your relationship started in a love cycle, but it's probably in a fear cycle now—too much of the time.

Both cycles have the same structure. Both have four words: two circles and two arrows. The circles are feelings, and the arrows are actions. We speak of fear circles and fear arrows, versus love circles and love arrows. Our love cycle is:

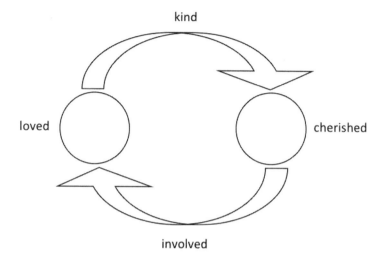

The circles in our love cycle are "loved" and "cherished"—the opposites of "abandoned" and "intimidated." Your love circles are your dreams—the ways you'd each like to feel. They are probably the opposite of your fear circles.

Like Cupid, your love arrow touches your partner's heart. It's probably the opposite of your fear arrow. Your fear arrow is their nightmare; your love arrow is their dream. When your partner feels loved, they become loving, and love you back.

I ask myself, "What would make Deborah feel cherished?" It's doing nice things, saying sweet things, having a warm presence. My love arrow is kindness—the opposite of getting angry. If you need help, exercise 22 can help you figure out your love arrow.

Your partner has a love arrow too. They can do things that really touch your heart and make you feel that your dream is coming true. You'll know you're in your love cycle when these things are happening.

Deborah makes me feel loved by staying involved. For me, that's her love arrow. It's the opposite of withdrawing. I feel loved when Deborah is willing to talk about something difficult. If you need help, exercise 23 can help you figure out your partner's love arrow.

The four words of our love cycle are kind, cherished, involved, and loved.

As before, each word leads to the next. When you're feeling good, it's easy to shoot your love arrow—same for your partner. Good feelings lead to loving actions, which lead to more good feelings. This is a "virtuous cycle"—the opposite of a vicious cycle. If you need help seeing this, exercise 24 can help you diagram your love cycle.

When you're in your love cycle, you don't need fight or flight because you're not feeling threatened. You're naturally generous and open. You're both more relaxed, more giving, more loving, more fun. When Deborah feels cherished and I feel loved, things are good.

WHO GOES FIRST?

In fear cycles many people argue about who goes first. People fight about "who started it," and about who should apologize first. In love cycles these fights disappear. Fairness isn't a problem when you're in your love cycle.

The easiest way to move from your fear cycle to your love cycle is to go first yourself. Don't insist they go first. Go ahead and do things to make your partner feel loved. Don't demand that they reciprocate right away. That demand will just spin you right back into your fear cycle. Your partner will probably withdraw (in one way or another). In fact, demand/withdraw is one of the most common fear cycles.

If I were to demand that Deborah stay involved, it wouldn't work. Whether or not she was involved a moment before, my demand would make her pull back. Mistakenly, I could conclude she wasn't willing to be involved, but that would overlook my role in scaring her away. By contrast, when I'm kind, Deborah responds by naturally being involved. It's easiest to change my own behavior first, and see whether that changes hers.

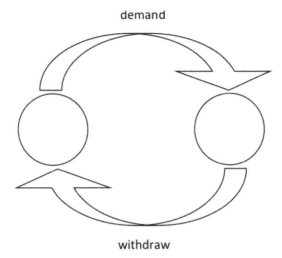

demand

withdraw

Sadly, it doesn't always work. For some couples, love arrows aren't reciprocated. It's possible that no matter what you do, no matter how long you do it, your partner won't change their part. If so, you've got some difficult decisions to make. You might want to consider whether "giving too much"/"giving too little" is your fear cycle. Giving too much can be a form of fight (moving toward); giving too little is a form of flight (moving away.) If this is your fear cycle, you may need to stop giving so much.

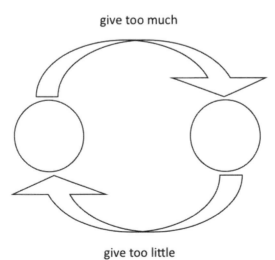

give too much

give too little

Do your part to reduce your fear cycle. Do your part to create your love cycle. Hopefully, your love cycle will emerge as your fear cycle recedes.

ALL FOUR WORDS TOGETHER

As you consider the four words of your love cycle, you'll see that each of the words leads to the next. You'll also notice that the two pairs of words resonate with each other. The loving feelings go together and the loving actions go together.

When Deborah feels cherished, I feel loved. When I feel loved, Deborah feels cherished. These two feelings resonate; they produce each other and amplify each other. Think about that resonance between the two of you. When that resonance happens, enjoy it. Give thanks for it—that's how you want to live.

Your loving actions resonate with each other too. The more you do loving things, the more your partner does loving things back. The kinder I am, the more involved Deborah is. The more involved Deborah is, the kinder I am—another lovely combination. The reciprocity of loving behaviors causes them to increase naturally. That's the delight of a love cycle: good things lead to more good things.

Deborah and I have a sweet example of this. A few times—not on any special occasion—I have left a set of little notes around the house stating my appreciation for various things that Deborah does. In the kitchen my note read, "Thanks for making scrumptious food for us so often." In the laundry room, on a wall, "Thanks for repainting our walls such a lovely color." I wrote about a dozen notes altogether.

I thought that I really should have written them on some lovely paper, but I didn't. I used the yellow notepad that was on my desk. I was worried that the presentation wasn't going to be nice enough, but I told myself to just go ahead and do the notes—not wait until everything was perfect.

I usually have trouble keeping things secret. I often give Deborah presents on the day I buy them. I felt the urge to tell her about the notes and set her off on a treasure hunt, but I decided that she'd prefer the opposite. She'd prefer that I not tell her and just let her find them. So I didn't say anything. I was patient and waited, even though it was hard for me, it felt like the right thing to do.

The next day I was sitting at my desk when Deborah came over to me overjoyed. "Honey! I found this note in the kitchen! Thank you! Thank you so much!" She was really touched and really happy. At that point, she thought I had only left one note, she didn't suspect there were others.

A little later in the day, she found a second note. Again she found me and told me how happy she was. She added, "It's so wonderful that you see me. It's wonderful that you see all the things I do." I was glad she felt so happy, although I was a little surprised. I make a point of telling her that I appreciate the particular things she does every day, usually more than once. But I realized that it touches Deborah differently when it's in writing.

Deborah has kept these little notes for years. She puts them in special places where she can see them. I guess they're reminders that I see her, appreciate her, and love her. For her they're part of feeling cherished.

Her joy when she found the notes really made me feel wonderful. I felt her love very strongly. I felt like I did something that touched her, and that she was truly glad to be with me. It was a love cycle moment. She felt cherished, I felt loved. We both felt great.

SAVING YOUR RELATIONSHIP

To save your relationship you have to overcome your fear cycle--again and again. It's not possible to end your fear cycle once and for all, but it is possible to be more skillful at getting out of it—and not getting into it in the first place. That's what it takes to stay together and be happy.

The first way to overcome your fear cycle is by remembering it. Remember you four words. When you see one of those words, look for the others. Remember that these words cause one another. Also, remember they are not the solution.

The second way to overcome your fear cycle is not reacting. When you feel triggered, stop yourself. Hold back your usual fight or flight. Remember your fear arrow; and don't shoot it. If you do, stop, change something, and apologize.

The third way to overcome your fear cycle is soothing your own feelings. Remember your circle; calm yourself when you feel that way.

Fear cycles have momentum. Changing that takes insight, intention and effort. But this is a make-it-or-break-it situation. To be happy, you have to break out of your fear cycle. It's that simple.

Making Your Dreams Come True

You two can make your dreams come true. Here's how: Remember your partner's dream. Figure out your love arrows. Shoot them. A lot.

There are four lovely times of day for this:

- When you wake up
- When the first person leave for the day
- When the second person comes home
- When you go to sleep

Each of these is a perfect time a hug, a kiss, some loving words, some compliment, some appreciation, some kindness.

Make these habits. When you can, make a little more love in your life. Remember the words of your love cycle. Write them somewhere. Try to make these happen every day. Your love cycle has momentum too. When you make your partner feel loved, they'll act a lot nicer.

↓ ↓ ↓

In this chapter, you've considered your dreams—what you really want. These dreams are the opposite of the hurt and lonely feelings in your fear cycle. You've found a word for each of your dreams and put them in the hearts of your fear cycle.

You've also made a new diagram of your love cycle. Overcoming your fear cycle is necessary; so is recreating your love cycle. As you create your love cycle—where each of you feels good and makes the other feel good—you create the life of your dreams. One view of that is:

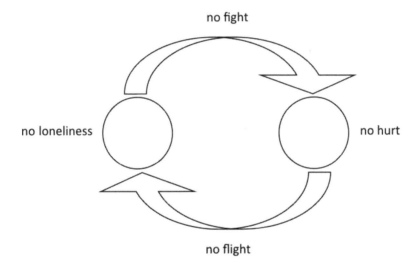

In the next chapter we'll talk about how to ask your partner to change.

CHAPTER NINE

ASKING YOUR PARTNER TO CHANGE

When love and skill work together, expect a masterpiece.

—John Ruskin

After changing your part of the cycle, you may want to ask your partner to change theirs. It's important to do this well. That's what we'll cover in this chapter.

OF COURSE YOU DON'T LIKE THEIR ARROW

Of course you don't like your partner's fear arrow. As far as you're concerned it's the worst thing they do. In severe circumstances this arrow can be a deal breaker. If your partner is physically abusive, repeatedly unfaithful, or addicted to something dangerous, you might be much better off without them.

But in less severe circumstances, their arrow isn't necessarily a reason to end the relationship. Nobody's perfect; there's always going to be something you don't like. One partner might be too intense; another not intense enough. One might be too proud, another not proud enough. The question is whether the good outweighs the bad.

Deborah can be more fearful than I like. Although she's very courageous at work, sometimes at home she lacks confidence. She can freeze up, withdraw, and seem cold. I don't like these moments. But when I consider Deborah's loyalty, her devotion, her honesty, her emotional depth, her generosity, her kindness, her charity, her caretaking, her beauty, and her hard work, the whole deal seems way worth it. There's a lot more good than bad.

I can be more severe and angry than Deborah likes. There are situations when I react too harshly. I can come across as uncaring or condescending. Deborah wishes I were different at these times. I do too. But she values other things about me. I'm loyal, hardworking, and faithful. I'm diligent, responsible, and trustworthy. I can be very understanding and empathic. I'm a good communicator and I think deeply about human situations.

Deborah also feels that the good outweighs the bad. So we're glad we're together. We appreciate the good about each other; we accept some of the bad. But we also ask each other to change some of the bad.

You Can't Make Someone Change

There's a very basic idea that we all need to accept: You can't make someone else change. No one has that ability. People who are imprisoned, people whose lives are threatened—those people can be forced to change. But you wouldn't want anything like that. In a loving relationship, you don't force your partner to change. All you can do is ask your partner to change. That's a big difference.

Your partner's willingness (or not) affects your happiness together. If they are willing to change, be grateful—and let them know. You might say something like, "When you're open to my feedback it makes me feel you really care. Thank you." Don't let this thought go unspoken. Let them know you appreciate their willingness to listen, to understand, and to do something about your concern.

On the other hand, perhaps no matter what you say, your partner isn't willing to change at all. Some people are like that. Some say, "I am the way I am. That's the way I've always been. You knew this was the way I was. I'm too old to change." It's possible that your partner is plain and simply unwilling to change anything.

If so, you've got some work to do. First, make sure you're not contributing to their stubbornness. Then, learn how to make SMART requests. Then, do this for a few months. If they're still refusing to cooperate, you'll need to decide whether to live with their stubbornness—or not. And if so, how to do it.

REMEMBER: DON'T SHOOT YOUR ARROW

Changing your part of the cycle is the easiest place to start. If you decide to change something, you can. There's nothing stopping you. You don't have to do any persuading. Your partner will probably appreciate the change.

You can restrain your arrow, or soothe the feelings in your circle. You can remember your family history and understand your sensitivity. You can reframe your partner's arrow, understand the feelings in their circle, or have compassion for their background. Any of these might help. Once you've done these, let's talk about asking your partner to change.

The most important error to avoid is: shooting your arrow to get them to stop shooting theirs. Many people try this; don't be one of them. Your arrow is the worst possible way to get them to change. It just accelerates your fear cycle.

Use your diagram to see what this error would be like for you. How might you, mistakenly, have used your arrow to try to stop their arrow? Review some situations when you've tried to get them to change. Look for ways in which you may have shot your arrow. If you can find some, that's good. You're seeing your part of the problem. From now on, use different ways.

SET UP A DISCUSSION

When you want your partner to change something, you first need to make a time to talk. You can't have one of these discussions on the fly. You can't do it while you're doing something else. You need undivided attention and willingness to listen. Agreeing on a time to talk is a way of establishing this consent. You want a time with no phones, no screens, and no kids. Make an appointment for that. I say, "Honey, there's something I want to talk to you about. When's a good time?" You need your version of that request.

I'd suggest starting with short appointments of ten to twenty minutes. It's easier to agree to a short talk than a long one. If your partner can't talk right away, that's okay. Let them choose the time. It doesn't need to be immediately. I'd rather have full attention tomorrow than preoccupied-listening today.

If your partner won't even agree to talk, you might need the help of a couples therapist. See Resources for Getting Professional Help.

When you do sit down to talk, make a "soft start." Begin with a soft voice. Start on a positive note. Say something pleasant. If you can't think of anything, say, "Thanks for sitting down with me," or "Thanks for taking time to talk." Any other compliments would be nice, too.

Next, state your intention. It's going to sound something like, "There's something I want to talk to you about. It's a problem I'm having. I hope we can talk about it and find a way to make it better." Even before mentioning the topic, state your positive intention for the conversation.

The reason for a soft start is to create a receptive, open-minded listener. The opposite approach—a harsh start—almost always puts the other person in a defensive, closed-minded stance. That's not what you want. You want open-hearted, willing to cooperate, concerned, thoughtful, and caring. Do your best to start that way.

If they do get defensive, you need to pause. There's no point in proceeding right then. You're not going to get through when they're defensive. Instead, try to repair the conversation. See if you can shift the mood. If you can't, you might as well stop for now. You're going to have to talk about this later. Don't keep hammering away. Don't spin into a criticism/defensiveness cycle. Don't escalate. Calm things down somehow, and see if you can agree to talk again later. If you can't even agree on that, you might state your desire to resume another time. Or maybe just say it to yourself. "We'll talk about this later." "I'll bring it up another time."

When your partner is willing to talk, here are the topics to cover: your frustration, your unmet need, your background, what you'd like (if you could have it all), and your specific requests. These form the acronym: FUBAR.

Asking Your Partner to Change   117

Frustration
Unmet Need
Background
All
Requests

Each of these corresponds to a part of your diagram.

FRUSTRATION: THEIR ARROW

First say what frustrates you. It's either something they're doing (and you wish they wouldn't) or something they're not doing (and you wish they would.) Don't make this part too long. Be clear, but don't elaborate. Don't give too many examples. Don't try to prove your point. For instance, I might say, "I don't like it when you get silent and don't have anything to say."

UNMET NEED: YOUR CIRCLE

The frustration is about your partner. Now shift to yourself. Your unmet need is something about you. It's something you need that you're not getting. It's explains why this frustration is so important to you.

I might say, "When you get silent, I feel all alone. I want to feel part of a team. I want to feel like we're working together. I want to feel partnered and loved." By talking about my unmet need, I'm acknowledging that this is an issue for me. I'm saying that these needs of mine are not all about Deborah. I'm saying that I've had these needs in other settings too. This is called "owning" the issue.

This shift—from talking about her to talking about me—is very important. When I talk about my frustration, it's debatable. Perhaps Deborah would say that she's not really getting silent. Perhaps she'd argue that it's not true that she doesn't have anything to say. We might disagree; we might even have a big argument about who was right.

But when I shift to my need, there's nothing to debate. I'm the one who knows my feelings and my needs. I'm the authority on that topic. Talking about your partner leads to debate; talking about yourself doesn't.

BACKGROUND: YOUR HOUSE

Most unmet needs are long-standing. Take a moment to trace the history of yours. See how long you've felt this way. The earlier you can remember the better. Unmet needs are usually part of the house in your diagram.

When you talk about your background, you let your partner off the hook. This almost always makes partners less defensive—and more compassionate. When they don't feel blamed and attacked, they'll want to help you more.

My background is that I yearned to feel loved, yet often felt alone. In high school, I remember how awful I felt about not having a girlfriend. In junior high, I remember feeling horrible when I was shunned by a friend. Even as a child I never felt really loved by my parents the way I wanted.

I could say to Deborah, "Feeling loved has always been something I've wanted and never had. It runs all the way back to my childhood. Even as a child I felt empty, alone, sad, and hopeless." This lets Deborah relax because the intensity of my need is not all her fault; it's something I've carried a long time. Yes, I'm frustrated when her behavior touches that old wound. But no, the wound is not all her doing.

This kind of sharing will probably be a big relief to your partner. It usually helps them understand you, care about you, and be willing help.

WHAT YOU TRULY WANT: YOUR HEART

Now shift to what you want. Turn your frustration into a request. Your frustration is something in the past that felt bad. Now think about something in the future that would feel good. That's your request. Shift from complaining about a past "bad," to asking for a future "good." "I don't like it when you get angry," becomes, "I'd like it if you'd stay calm." "I don't like it when you withdraw," becomes, "I'd like it if you'd stay involved."

These are global, all-encompassing requests. They mean, "I'd like it if you stayed calm, all the time, so I could always feel safe." Or "I'd like it if you stayed involved all the time, so I could feel always loved."

These needs are the heart in your diagram. They are what you really want. They are what you yearn for. This is what would heal all the pain of your fear cycle. This is called your "global request." This is what you'd want in a perfect world—if you could "have it all."

It's helpful to say this global request out loud, so you can both hear it. You both need to realize that this global request is the end of the journey, but it's not the next step. Yes, we all have our deepest longings—but those things can't happen fully right away. Instead, we take steps in that direction. Over time, many of those steps will get us there. We can't expect the destination at the beginning.

SPECIFIC REQUESTS: THEIR LOVE ARROW

The next step is to request something specific you would like your partner to do. This will be a new and better arrow. It will be a love arrow—part of your love cycle.

There's another acronym for how to make requests that work. That acronym is SMART. Smart requests are:

Specific
Measurable
Achievable
Relevant
Time-Limited

Many people don't make smart requests, and—for that reason—many requests don't work. Many wind up right back at frustration. But if you start making smart requests, your chances of progress will be much higher. It takes a little practice, but it's worth it. As you read through each of the qualities of smart requests, you may see some of the mistakes you've been making.

The most frequent mistake is called, "Knock it off!" To make this mistake, you think about what's frustrating you, and you ask them to stop it. You might say, "Please, stop doing this thing I dislike so much." You might think this is straightforward, honest, and direct. Yes, it is—but it's not very smart. It's not specific. It's not measureable. It's almost never achievable. And it's not time-limited. This type of request is guaranteed to fail.

Deborah doesn't like my anger. We both know that. Her knock-it-off request would be, "Stop being angry at me." Well, I understand her point. I'm not against it. I'm willing to work on it. But that request is not likely to turn out well. Let's say I succeed at not being angry nine times in a row. Then, on the tenth time, I fail and get angry. That's the time she'll notice. She'll think I didn't do what she asked, and we'll both be frustrated.

MAKE SPECIFIC REQUESTS

A knock-it-off request is general, but people get angry in specific ways. There's screaming, raising one's voice, feeling angry inside, and showing anger in one's face. There are furrowed brows and tight lips. Deborah would probably like all these things changed. But nobody can change them all at once.

A specific request addresses one behavior at a time. Sure, a few weeks from now Deborah might make another request about another behavior. But one specific thing at a time is all that most people can do.

Sometimes I think I can manage two self-improvement projects at a time. But that's my limit. I'm just not capable of remembering and managing very many at a time. Over the months and years, I'm willing to agree to make many changes, but I won't succeed at doing them all at once.

Here are some of the specific requests we implemented when we were working on my anger. For a while, when I was angry, we would talk on our stairway. Deborah would stand on the third step, while I stayed on the landing. It made her feel safer that I wasn't looming over her.

Then there was a while when we would talk about problems with Deborah in the living room and me in the dining room—with our foyer in between us. It made her feel safer that we had some distance between us.

We also used time-out. Either of us could call time-out at any time: immediate stop, no questions asked, and a thirty-minute break to calm down.

These plans were very specific. When I did them, Deborah felt like I was taking her sensitivity into account. I got credit for handling anger in a way that made her feel safer.

ASK FOR SOMETHING MEASUREABLE

The request, "Don't be angry" isn't measureable. Whenever you ask someone to not do something, it's hard to notice when the "not-doing" happens. We notice things that happen much more easily than we notice things that don't happen.

If I try to not get angry, I'll probably succeed many times a day. I might calm myself by saying, "It's no big thing." "I don't need to make a fuss about this." "It's not the end of the world." Suppose I succeeded twice in the morning before I went to work. The dirty cat bowl is no big deal; the dishes in the sink aren't a problem. Then, driving to work, I think about something else that bugs me, but I decide I don't need to call Deborah about this right now. I know this isn't a good moment in the day for talking about problems.

Then we see each other for lunch. I choose to ask about her day, and not raise the problem. I don't want to talk about a problem in the middle of the work day. It might spoil our lunch, and Deborah might think of it as anger.

So, time after time, I've honored Deborah's request to not to get angry. But Deborah might not have noticed any of these. She might just think that life was going fine, and have no idea that I'd been restraining my tendency to talk about problems right away.

That might continue until I slipped up. Perhaps in the evening I want to ask her to change something. She could think of that as me being angry at her. And now, for the first time that day, she'd notice anger. And she could think: I asked him not to be angry at me, and here he is, on the first day, getting angry at me already.

I would have gotten no credit for all my successes, because she wouldn't have noticed any of them. I'd get busted for my one failure, because that's all she'd notice. This is a general principle: If you make negative requests—where you ask someone to not do something— you'll only notice failure.

And negative requests are so much harder for people to do. With a negative request, your partner has to be watchful all day. They have to continually monitor their behavior, and restrain themselves when- ever necessary. They're on duty whenever they're awake. That's a lot of time, and a lot of concentration.

By contrast, a positive request—where you ask someone to do something—is so much easier. They only have to do it a few times a day. They don't have to focus on it 24/7. It is much easier to for them to succeed at, and for you to notice their successes.

ASK FOR SOMETHING THAT YOUR PARTNER CAN DO

For a request to succeed it's got to be achievable. Your partner's got to be able to do it. If you ask for something impossible, you already know it's not going to happen. You know they'll fail; you know you'll be frustrated.

It's shocking how many people make requests that are not achiev- able. The usual error is to ask for an impossibly large step. For me that would sound like, "Honey, when I'm angry, I'd like for you to mir- ror back what I've said, and check that you got it right. And then ask me if there's any more. And then, when I'm done, validate my points and tell me what makes sense to you about what I've said. And let me know that you can understand that I'm angry, and why I'd be angry."

These aren't necessarily bad ideas. But when I string all of them together, it's far too much to ask—especially at a moment when I know she's feeling intimidated.

We all need to make requests that are much smaller and much easier to do. You want steps that are small enough so your partner will be willing to try, and have a good chance of succeeding. You will both feel a lot better with successful small steps than with unsuccessful big ones. Here's an example of a time we got that right:

Deborah would often get silent right in the middle of a discussion. It was very frustrating to me. It seemed like she was unwilling to talk—and not willing to let me know she was done talking. It really left me hanging. I'd hope she was just pausing, so I'd wait. And wait. And wait. And she wouldn't say anything. I wanted her to continue the discussion. If she disagreed with something, I wanted her to say so. I wanted her to let me know what was going on with her. I didn't want her to just get silent, drop out, and stonewall.

But my request was much more achievable than all that. I asked her—at the moments when she paused—to say the words, "I'm thinking." That was the whole request. It was small, easy and do-able.

She agreed to do it, although it seemed unnecessary to her. She thought it was obvious that she was thinking. What else could she be doing? Well, I had made up a lot worse possibilities. I'd made up that she was furious, or terrified, or couldn't stand the discussion. When she said, "I'm thinking," I felt a lot better. She was saying something, rather than being silent. She was letting me know what was going on. It confirmed the best possibility, not the worst. She hadn't dropped out and withdrawn; she just needed some time to think.

This worked very well for us, and we even came up with a variation on it. Sometimes she'd forget to say, "I'm thinking." So I'd ask her, "Are you thinking?" She'd laugh and say, "Yes." That worked fine too.

This is a good example of an achievable request. Even when she was feeling uncomfortable, overwhelmed, or at a loss for words, she could still say, "I'm thinking." That little change made a big difference.

ASK FOR SOMETHING RELEVANT

Of course, your requests should be relevant to your needs. Deborah asked me to handle my anger more thoughtfully, so she'd feel less intimidated. I asked her to say the words, "I'm thinking," so I wouldn't feel abandoned. You want your partner to understand the connection between this specific request and your larger need. You want them to help because they care about you.

MAKE TIME-LIMITED REQUESTS

People are much more willing to try something for a little while, than commit to a permanent change for the rest of their lives. You need your partner's willingness. Yes, you'd probably like this request to be forever. But you'll get much less resistance if you propose a brief trial period. You might try a week, two weeks or a month—depending on how frequently the behavior occurs and how hard it is to do. The harder the request is, the shorter the time limit. Sometimes when it's a big change, I suggest people limit their request to "the next time." If that time works, maybe it will create some hope and some new momentum.

I had asked, "The next time we're talking and you need to pause, would you please say, 'I'm thinking'?" Deborah agreed for one time only. But when that one time happened, we both loved it. It was funny. It was helpful. So we decided it was a keeper. That small request— one time only—led to a big change.

Another type of time-limit is, "When I do A, would you please do B?" When Deborah says, "Let me finish," she wants me to say, "Okay," and stop talking. I've agreed to this; I think it's a good idea. I know I can talk too much, and she can talk too little. I'm in favor of better balance. So this plan lets her get some airspace whenever she wants. It's much easier for me to be quiet when she asks, than it would be to monitor the balance of every conversation.

In this format, your partner doesn't need to do B all the time, only when you do A. That might make changing a lot easier.

↓ ↓ ↓

You can't make someone change; you can ask them to change. Of course, you want them to change their arrow. But be wise about how you ask. Don't use your arrow to get them to change theirs. Instead, make a time to talk. Make a smart request. Be patient. Hope for the best.

In the next chapter, we'll talk about common problems that many couples face. You'll see the fear cycle that can develop with each—and suggestions for getting out of those cycles.

CHAPTER TEN

COMMON PROBLEMS COUPLES FACE

The meeting of two personalities is like the contact of two chemical substances:
If there is any reaction, both are transformed.

—Carl Jung, *Modern Man in Search of a Soul*

All couples have differences in preferences, habits, upbringings, and personalities. Not all differences are problems; some lead to warmth, humor and affection. But some differences lead to bickering—or serious fighting. Some make people feel profoundly alone. Some lead to divorce. These are differences that have become escalated, polarized fear cycles.

In this chapter we'll describe a number of these:

Sex
Anger
Money
In-laws
Parenting
Closeness
Work and Chores
Being on Time
Neatness

Don't feel bad if you identify with one or more. All couples have problems. The goal is to talk about these conflicts, understand one another, and work together to get out of the fear cycle so you can make progress.

Your Sexual Relationship

The most frequent problem that brings people to sex therapy is discrepant desire—when one person wants sex more than the other. Often this is a genuine biological difference between two people. It's not necessarily due to other problems in the relationship. It's not necessarily about a turn-off. It's not necessarily about someone's sexual history. Sure, any of those could affect desire. But often discrepant desire is just a physiological difference.

Sometimes this isn't much of a problem. Some couples evolve a compromise frequency that feels okay to both people. Some couples develop variety in their lovemaking so that the lower desire partner can participate more or less. For many couples this is no big deal.

But discrepant desire can become a fear cycle where wanting-more and wanting-less lead to threatened and rejected:

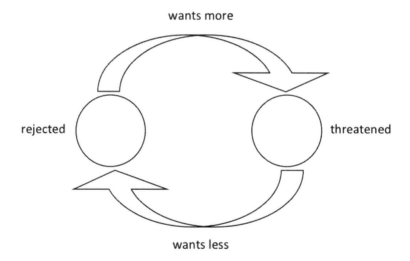

If your partner wants more, you're likely to feel threatened in some way. Maybe you feel bad that you don't have more desire. Maybe you feel bad that you're not satisfying your partner. Maybe you fear that your partner will be driven to infidelity. Maybe you feel pressured to give in, and then ambivalent about doing so. Maybe you feel guilty about your ambivalence, and fearful that your partner will be displeased. There are a lot of things you could worry about. Unfortunately, when worried, you're less romantic, not more. So you say you're not interested.

Then your partner can feel rejected. They wanted to connect with you, and you turned them down. They're disappointed; you can understand that. But it becomes a problem when feeling rejected makes them act needier. Then they want to connect even more.

That's when you're off to the races. As they press for more connection, you feel more threatened and then they feel even more rejected. That's when discrepant desire is a problem. Some couples have hurtful fights about this. Some have growing disconnection that erodes their relationship.

If you have this fear cycle, use this book. You could start by focusing on your partner's feeling threatened—or rejected. You certainly don't want them to feel that way. Talk to them about this with compassion; see what you can do to change this feeling. "Honey, I certainly don't want to you feel threatened." "Honey, I certainly don't want you to feel rejected." "Let's figure out what we can do about this."

How You Handle Anger

In most relationships, one partner gets angrier than the other. Often, like us, one gets loud while the other gets quiet. This is a legitimate difference. As with desire, this difference is perfectly reasonable and not necessarily a problem. Yes, people are different, and that's no big deal. But, like with sex, it's a problem if it becomes a fear cycle where loud and quiet lead to scared and abandoned.

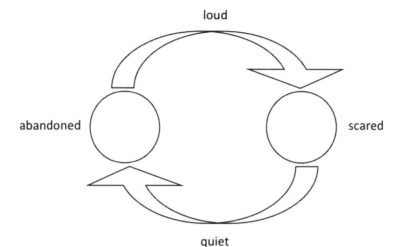

The scared person gets quiet to calm things down. But that makes the loud person feel abandoned, and so they cry out in protest—loud protest. You need to get out of this cycle.

One possible way is meeting in the middle on volume. The loud person calms down and talks more quietly; the quiet one speaks up and uses a stronger voice. If you revert back to the old pattern, try to change it. If you don't succeed at changing it, call time-out to give yourselves a break.

Is it okay to change a long-standing pattern, just because it's uncomfortable for your partner? My opinion is yes, within reason. Changing your volume is a reasonable compromise.

Don't be stubborn; don't be unwilling. Don't say, "That's just the way I am." If you do, you'll seem very uncaring and unloving.

Instead, remember your partner's feelings. Loud makes them feel scared. Quiet makes them feel abandoned. When they're loud, they're probably feeling abandoned. When they're quiet, they're probably feeling scared. Think about each of your childhoods. That's when you learned about loud and quiet.

Your Relationship with Money

One frequent money problem is between a saver and a spender. In Aesop's fable "The Ant and the Grasshopper" the ant works all summer saving food for the winter while the grasshopper spends the summer singing and playing. Come winter, the grasshopper has to beg the ant for food. Aesop felt that saving was better, but like with most polarities, there is virtue on both sides. A blend of both is probably better than all or nothing.

To a saver, enjoying the moment is less important saving for the future. But spenders focus on present enjoyment. They think, "Life is short," and, "You only live once."

These two people can polarize easily. One thinks: I have to save a lot, because they never save anything. The other thinks: I have to argue for the good things in life, otherwise we'd never have any of them. When this becomes a fear cycle, saver and spender, lead to feeling insecure and deprived.

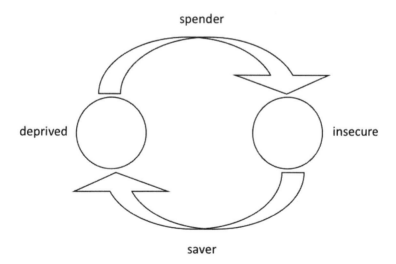

One way out of this fear cycle is to understand each other's dreams, and the origin of those dreams. One type of dream is, "I want it because I never had it." Another type of dream is "I want it because I've always had it."

Some people want a beautiful house because they never had one. They grew up in much more humble circumstances, yet yearned for greater wealth and success. Achieving this goal feels like the fulfillment of a lifelong desire. Other people want a beautiful house because that's how they grew up. That's what they're accustomed to, that's the lifestyle they expect.

Your goal should be a reasonable compromise of agreed-upon saving and agreed-upon spending. Some people use a "three-pot" system to address this—dividing their money among one joint pot and two separate pots. They make an agreement how much of each income goes into which pots. They decide together about spending and saving the joint pot. They decide individually about the separate pots.

Dealing with In-Laws

Some of the most intense fear cycles are about in-laws. Family problems can be very challenging because you may have to deal with some very difficult people. You may have some problems with your partner's parents; or your partner may have some problems with your parents. This can become a strain on your relationship with each other.

It can become a fear cycle very quickly. Suppose you have a problem with your in-laws and they have a problem with you. You complain about them and they complain about you—and your partner gets caught in the middle.

Your partner feels defensive when you criticize his or her parents. They may try to tell you that their parents are good, or well-meaning. They may say you need to give them the benefit of the doubt, or not take their comments so personally. They may try to smooth things over between you and their parents, and make peace between all parties.

But when they're being the peacemaker, it feels like they don't have your back. When they're in a "neutral" role, it feels like they're not on your side. As they defend and accommodate their family, you become pretty powerless. When they're invested in being "the good child," they can't stand up for you or take any position against their family's wishes.

So you're left hanging. Without your partner's backing, you're powerless. There's nothing you can do to change the family situation. Maybe you feel angry or resentful, frustrated or abandoned. Maybe you blame their family for the difficulties they're making in your relationship.

The two of you are experiencing a polarization between blaming and placating. Your partner is placating his or her family by trying to make peace; you're blaming his or her family for what they're doing wrong.

You each have valid points. Peace is good; change is good. But when you two spin into a fear cycle, it's all bad. You wind up feeling more and more powerless; they feel more and more defensive.

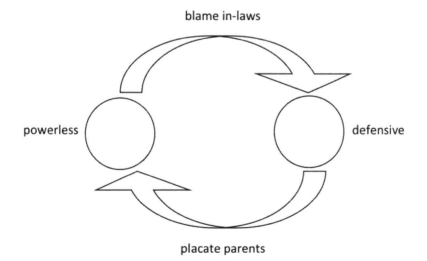

blame in-laws

powerless   defensive

placate parents

134 LOVE CYCLES, FEAR CYCLES

If this describes you, your most important task is to fight the polarization. Don't criticize your in-laws because your partner defends them so much. Or, the other way around, don't side with your parents because you think your partner's being unfair. Stop compensating for each other; stop pushing each other to extremes. Together, you need to discuss a middle way that is neither blaming nor placating.

Start by changing the parts you can. Change your own thinking. Don't let yourself think of anyone as all-good or all-bad. Of course everyone has some bad traits and some good ones. None of your parents are perfect, and none are without redeeming qualities.

To regain some balance, lean into the opposite part of your cycle. If you tend to blame, find ways you can appreciate your in-laws. Think this out; then put it in words. Find an opportunity to let them know what you appreciate. Write them, tell them. If you tend to placate, find ways you can disagree with your parents. Maybe there are some things you'll decline to do, or suggest a new way to do them.

When you talk to each other be mindful about polarizing. Make a point of affirming whatever you can about your partner's point of view. "Sure, I understand why you don't like that." "Yes, it makes sense to me that you don't want to upset them." Then, intentionally steer your conversation toward the middle. Talk about things you can agree to do with your family. Find things that are reasonable and respectful yet still reflect your own needs and your own way of doing things. Explore compromise, give-and-take, and creative solutions.

WORKING TOGETHER AS PARENTS

The most frequent parenting polarization is strict versus lenient. When this becomes a fear cycle it looks like:

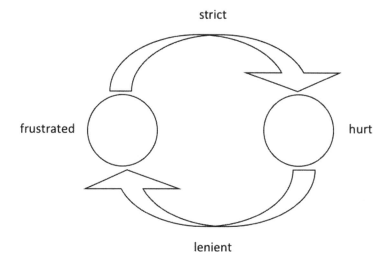

If you think your partner is too strict, there's a tendency for you to identify with the child (or children) and feel bad yourself. You think your child is being hurt unnecessarily and that hurts you. You want the best for the children and you wince when something bad happens to them. When you can, you try to make it up to them. You comfort them, you do something nice with them, or you give them some little treat. You make clear that you have a different opinion about what happened. If the same behavior happens with you, you don't respond as strictly. Usually, the stricter your co-parent is, the more you compensate by being understanding and lenient.

On the other hand, if your partner is too lenient, you feel frustrated. Parenting is much more difficult when your co-parent is undermining you. You worry that the kids are getting spoiled, and that they won't grow up to be healthy adults. You're trying to provide healthy limits and consequences but getting no support. So you become stricter. You think: somebody's got to set some limits here. Somebody needs to establish some rules. We can't have the kids just running wild, doing whatever they want, disregarding what we tell them, disobeying and disrespecting us. That's not right.

As you know, this difference between you escalates. One of you gets stricter and stricter, and more and more frustrated. The other gets more and more lenient, and more and more hurt. It's a bad deal.

The cure involves having parenting conferences, negotiating, making agreements, and presenting a united front. First, you may want to come to some agreements about your parenting values and methods. I suggest looking over a few parenting books and choosing one. Read it, talk about it, and see what parts you want to try.

Then you need to step away from the kids and confer with each other. These little parenting conferences shouldn't be a big deal. You say something like, "Give us a minute, kids, we need to talk about this." Or, "We'll get back to you when we've decided what to do." Sometimes there's no time for discussion, but other times there is. You don't always need to respond right away. Those are the times when you can step aside and talk.

This is when you negotiate with each other. Does anything from your book apply to this situation? Use both of your opinions in the discussion. Make a decision you both can live with. Once you have an agreement, you return to the children with a united front:

> "We both agree that . . ."
> "Your father and I agree that . . ."
> "Your mother and I agree that . . ."

You want to say this often. It's good for your family.

THE CLOSENESS BETWEEN YOU

One of the most common fear cycles is between a pursuer and a distancer. It's a struggle about how much time to spend together versus apart, and how much "closeness" to have. The fear cycle is:

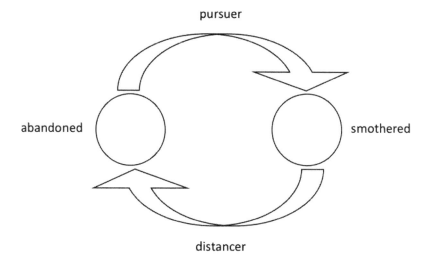

pursuer

abandoned   smothered

distancer

The pursuer wants more connection, so they frequently suggest doing things together: talking, being affectionate, going places and doing things. Unfortunately, this feels smothering to their partner. So the distancer pulls back. They need their own space. They need separate time. They need to do their own thing.

This is fine—to a degree. But a distancer pulls back so much that a pursuer feels abandoned. It can feel like your partner doesn't want to be with you. It's as if he or she would prefer being by themselves or with others.

So, the pursuer wants to talk about it, discuss the problem and solve it. They try to persuade the distancer to share what's really happening, and what's really important in the relationship. That, of course, feels even more smothering to the distancer. And the cycle is spinning.

The cure is straightforward. Pursuers: stop pursuing. It makes your partner feel smothered. It makes them distance more. Distancers: stop distancing. It makes your partner feel abandoned. It makes them pursue you more. That's not what you want.

Advice to pursuers: "If you love someone, let them go. If they come back to you, they're truly yours. If not, they never were." This isn't easy advice to follow, but it's essential. Clutching doesn't work; desperation isn't attractive.

Advice to distancers: Don't hurt your partner feelings. Don't make them feel abandoned, rejected and unwanted. That's not nice. Of course you need to work out a reasonable balance of together and apart. But stop arguing for "apart" so much. If you want to be in this relationship, lean into some significant together time and watch them lighten up. On the other hand, if you really don't want to be in this relationship, maybe it's time to tell your partner how you feel, so you can each decide how to proceed.

HANDLING WORK AND CHORES

Many couples struggle about how hard each one works. This includes how much each does at home, and how much each does at work. As traditional roles change, these disagreements can get quite intense.

There are different arrangements that could succeed; the same solution doesn't work for all couples. The key is making agreements by mutual consent. Two equal parties can agree to whatever division of labor they'd like. They can change those agreements as life circumstances evolve.

But a fear cycle develops when things get too far out-of-balance and one person is doing far too great a share of the work. That cycle looks like:

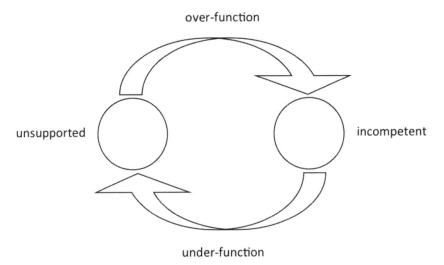

The person who over-functions is usually pretty busy and pretty stressed with all they have to do. They feel unsupported by their partner with all the pressure of work that needs to be done. Whether they need to earn more money, or do everything around the house, they know that someone's got to do it. So they get to work. That's nice in one way: the tasks get done. But it's often not so nice in another way: the relationship can deteriorate.

The person who under-functions also sees what has to be done, but steps back to reduce the stress. One values hard work and achievement, one values relaxation and enjoyment. Of course they each have a valid point. But one has to do so much because the other does so little; and one can do so little because the other does so much. As this cycle escalates these roles become more and more exaggerated.

It's tempting to see the hard worker as good and the slacker as bad. In fact, if you're in this fear cycle, you may fight about that very thing. The faults of the under-functioner are pretty clear. They're not doing their fair share. They're leaving their partner unsupported in many ways.

The solution centers on supporting your partner by helping with the work and stresses they face. This may involve taking on more responsibilities. It may also involve talking with your partner about the division of labor between you.

The faults of the over-functioner are subtler, but also problematic. These people are doing too much and, perhaps unintentionally, making their partner feel incompetent. Some also get critical, some get self-righteous, some play the martyr, and some make their partners feel guilty.

The solution is to stop doing more than your fair share—and deal with whatever problems result. You might need to have some serious discussions about changing responsibilities. It's likely that there will be substantial disagreement. This might involve some re-evaluation of the life-style you two want.

Over-functioning to avoid conflict is not the best long-term strategy; neither is under-functioning to avoid responsibility. Discussion, negotiation and teamwork are a better way.

DIFFERENCES ABOUT "BEING ON TIME"

In many couples, one person likes to be on time while the other doesn't seem to care. The more anxious person likes to be early while the more relaxed person thinks being early is unnecessary. In some relationships this is humorous. In others relationships this becomes a fight. The relaxed person can feel controlled; the anxious person can feel manipulated.

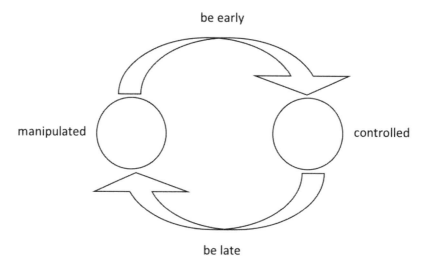

be early

manipulated   controlled

be late

Being told to hurry doesn't feel good. It makes the more-relaxed person feel controlled, criticized, harassed. Their more anxious partner seems impatient, irritated and unpleasant.

If you're the more relaxed person, it seems you're being told that your natural pace is not okay. It seems like your partner wants to change what you do and how you do it. Maybe this seems parental; maybe it feels demeaning. Maybe this kind of pressure makes you less efficient. Maybe you get distracted when your partner is irritated like this. Some people get resentful; some rebel. Some get even slower, and later.

The more anxious person often feels manipulated. They think their requests are reasonable. They want cooperation and harmony, not rushing, drama, and tension. But that's not what happens. Their requests don't work; the agreed-upon time doesn't happen. They feel manipulated. They think their partner isn't being straightforward and honest. They said they'd be ready, but they're not. They say one thing but do another. You can't trust them. They're unreliable. They don't keep their word.

This fear cycle can make life unpleasant. Every trip, every dinner party, every meeting, every religious service can start with a fight. That's no way to live. The way out of this fear cycle is meeting in the middle. No one wants their partner to feel manipulated or controlled. That's what needs to change. You've got to talk about this problem. You need to make a plan for how to do things differently. You need to try that plan and see how it works. You hope for a step forward.

Even this one little step may not work. If so, calm down. You'll need to talk again—but probably not in the heat of the moment. Sometime, before your next scheduled event, you need another plan. What can you each do to make the other's experience a little easier? Look for give-and-take.

How can you be less controlling? By offering to help? By making more flexible arrangements? By calming yourself down? By re-evaluating the consequences of being late—and realizing it's not as awful as you think?

How can you be less manipulative? What's the best thing to say when you know you're running late? Are there some preparations you could do earlier? Are there some things that others could do? Can you be direct about the time agreement you'd prefer? You two have to talk, you have to try different things, and you need some give-and-take.

CONFLICTS ABOUT NEATNESS

Some couples differ about neatness and messiness. Some couples work with each other about this difference, respecting each other's habits and preferences. But for other couples this can be a major aggravation and an ongoing battle. People can get very set in their ways about this.

When it becomes a fear cycle, one of you feels constrained and the other feels anxious. You two rub each other the wrong way, and the irritation happens many times a day.

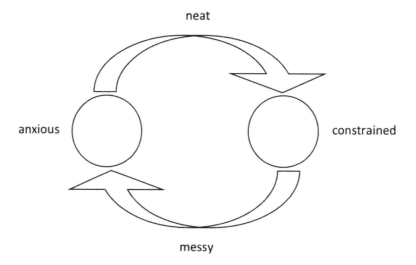

If your partner is the neat one, you probably feel very constrained. You can't do this, you must do that, you have to be careful where you put every little thing. You can't just relax and be yourself because everything needs to be "just so." Whether it's their complaints or their frustrated attitude, you know they disapprove of how you do things.

If your partner is the messy one, they're continually creating an environment that feels uncomfortable to you. Again and again they leave things out and don't put them away. They leave unfinished projects around. This is not the way you like your space—it makes you uncomfortable. You want a neat and organized space so you can be efficient and effective. But that's not what you've got.

At the extreme end of neatness is obsessive-compulsive disorder. At the extreme end of messiness is hoarding. But even in the milder ranges, these tendencies can be irritating, and you can end up making each other uncomfortable in your own home.

The worst problem is over-compensation, when you self-righteously do more of your style to balance out your partner. They're so messy that you have to keep everything especially neat. You have to enforce "a place for everything, and everything in its place." Or they're so neat that you have to create some lived-in-ness by leaving things around. It's easy to put each other down about this. "Neat freak" and "slob" are not just complaints, they're contempt. These put-downs say that your partner is not a good person—they're bad, they're wrong, they have a character defect. Couples can fight and bicker about this for decades. That's not a good plan.

Your difference is probably going to be a life-long. You probably can't make this problem go away entirely. The best you can hope for is discussion, understanding, and give-and-take. You need to be able to talk about this neat/messy difference. You need to share how this makes you feel—constrained, anxious, or however you'd describe it. You need to be able to see the cycle together, and how you both can wind up feeling bad. The fear cycle is your mutual enemy.

It might be helpful to understand each of your backgrounds and how your childhoods have influenced you. Was your home neat or messy? Did you like that, or not? How did you cope with it? Did you go along with it, did you rebel, or did you do it differently? Are you recreating your childhood environment now? Or are you creating the opposite? Sharing these insights with one another will help build understanding and compassion.

You can expect a lifelong process of adjustments. Yes, it's okay to ask each other to change. But you also have to accept some things about your partner that you don't like. That's called the paradox of acceptance and change: you need both. You can get partial improve-ments; you can get sincere attempts to change, and sincere attempts to accommodate your different needs. But you probably can't get a basic change in the person's style. Luckily that's not necessary. Nobody's perfect. You get to decide whether the good outweighs the bad. Is this something you can live with? For many people the answer is yes.

$$\downarrow\ \downarrow\ \downarrow$$

Any two people have differences. Some of these are easily handled, some aren't. We've discussed fear cycles that can happen about sex, anger, money, in-laws, parenting, closeness, work and chores, being on time, and neatness. Be grateful for the ones that aren't problems. If one or more of these is a problem, don't get discouraged. Take one at a time. Don't try to solve them all at once. Use this book. Work to understand the fear cycle, and get out of it. If you need help, get it.

All couples have fear cycles. Nobody wants them. Getting out of them takes work. But it's so worth it.

AFTERWORD

Here are some final thoughts on a healthy relationship. There are four key moments of the day to connect with each other warmly. They are: when you get up, when you leave the house, when you come home, and when you go to sleep. Those are important times to be sweet to each other. Touch your partner, and maybe give them a hug or a kiss. Say something nice. Four times every day. You'll find it adds up and makes a big contribution toward your happiness as a couple.

Once a day have a little chat. Sit down together for some uninterrupted time. Turn off the screens. Don't respond to the phone. Just hang out for a little while. Ask about each other's day. Make small talk. Talk about things of mutual interest. Ten to fifteen minutes might do it. If you have young children, the best time for this is right after the kids go to bed. Talk first, and do your own thing next.

Be careful not to let these conversations become arguments. Make three topics off-limits. Agree not to talk about (1) each other, (2) your relationship, and (3) problems between you. This way you can have a pleasant chat.

Distinguish talking about problems from chatting. Give them different names. You need to be able to do both, but keep them separate. Don't get confused about which you are doing. When you need to talk about problems, do it by appointment. Don't shift into problems in the middle of some other discussion.

Once a week do something interesting together, just the two of you. Once a quarter see if you can get away at least overnight. Make birthdays fun, make holidays enjoyable. These are not the time for problems.

Rabbi Hillel was asked to explain the Torah while standing on one foot. He said, "Do not do to others what you would not have them do to you."

Dr. John Gottman was asked to synthesize his thirty years of research on marriage into the most important advice for couples. He said, "Be nice."

EXERCISE
WORKBOOK

DO YOU PREFER FIGHT OR FLIGHT?

When things are bad, and the two of you are not getting along, and you're feeling upset, what are you more likely to do?

On each line, check one:

❏ Engage	or	❏ Disengage
❏ Approach	or	❏ Avoid
❏ Push forward	or	❏ Pull back
❏ Open up	or	❏ Shut down
❏ Talk more	or	❏ Talk less
❏ Talk now	or	❏ Talk later
❏ Get louder	or	❏ Get quieter
❏ Get more intense	or	❏ Get more subdued

If you have more checks in the first column, you prefer "fight."
If you have more checks in the second column, you prefer "flight."
So, what's your preference?

❏ Fight or **❏ Flight**

YOUR PARTNER'S PREFERENCE

When things are bad, and the two of you are not getting along, and your partner is upset, what is your partner more likely to do?

On each line, check one:

❏ Engage	or	❏ Disengage
❏ Approach	or	❏ Avoid
❏ Push forward	or	❏ Pull back
❏ Open up	or	❏ Shut down
❏ Talk more	or	❏ Talk less
❏ Talk now	or	❏ Talk later
❏ Get louder	or	❏ Get quieter
❏ Get more intense	or	❏ Get more subdued

If you have more checks in the first column, your partner prefers "fight." If you have more checks in the second column, your partner prefers "flight."

So, what's your partner's preference?

❏ Fight or **❏ Flight**

Are you two different? Does one of you prefer fight and the other prefer flight?

If so, proceed to **Exercise 3**.

Or

Are you two the same? Do you both prefer fight? Or both prefer flight?

If so, skip **Exercises 3–10**, and go to **Exercise 11**.

Exercise 3

PUT YOURSELVES ON THE DIAGRAM

Your Fear Cycle diagram will look like one of these.

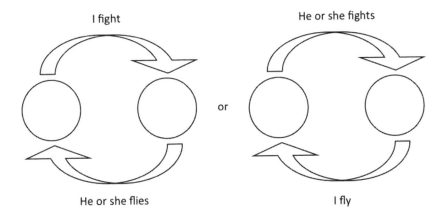

Put your names on the diagram below. The fighter goes on top; the flier goes on the bottom.

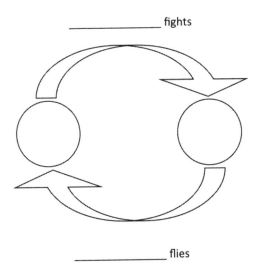

Fill in the blanks below with your names:

The more _____ fights, the more _____ flies.

The more _____ flies, the more _____ fights.

Could this be true?   ❏ yes ❏ no

Exercise 4

THE FIGHT IN YOUR RELATIONSHIP

How much of a problem are each of the behaviors listed below from the one who prefers fight? If your partner prefers fight, you'll know the answers. If you're the one who prefers fight, try to put yourself in your partner's shoes as you check the boxes.

	No problem	Moderate Problem		Big problem	
	0	1	2	3	4
Yelling	❏	❏	❏	❏	❏
Screaming	❏	❏	❏	❏	❏
Controlling	❏	❏	❏	❏	❏
Demanding	❏	❏	❏	❏	❏
Pressuring	❏	❏	❏	❏	❏
Pursuing	❏	❏	❏	❏	❏
Nagging	❏	❏	❏	❏	❏
Criticizing	❏	❏	❏	❏	❏
Accusing	❏	❏	❏	❏	❏
Blaming	❏	❏	❏	❏	❏
_____	❏	❏	❏	❏	❏

(add your own word)

Of your highest scores, which is the greatest problem?

Write the name of the one who fights in the first blank below. Put the worst way they fight in the second blank. For instance, "Abe yells," or "Alice controls."

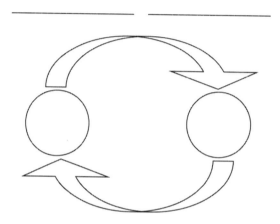

Exercise 5

THE FLIGHT IN YOUR RELATIONSHIP

How much of a problem are each of the behaviors listed below from the one who prefers flight? If your partner is the flier, you'll know the answers. If you're the flier, try to put yourself in your partner's shoes.

	No problem	Moderate Problem		Big problem	
	0	1	2	3	4
Withdrawing	❑	❑	❑	❑	❑
Distancing	❑	❑	❑	❑	❑
Avoiding	❑	❑	❑	❑	❑
Ignoring	❑	❑	❑	❑	❑
Shutting Down	❑	❑	❑	❑	❑
Defending	❑	❑	❑	❑	❑
Manipulating	❑	❑	❑	❑	❑
Being unreliable	❑	❑	❑	❑	❑
Playing victim	❑	❑	❑	❑	❑
_____	❑	❑	❑	❑	❑

(add your own word)

Of your highest scores, which is the greatest problem?

_____

Write the name of the one who flies in the first blank below. Put the worst way they fly in the second blank. For instance, "Ben withdraws," or "Barbara distances."

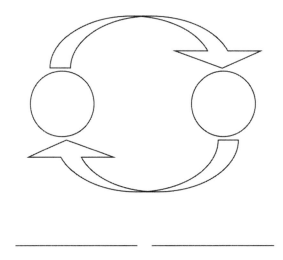

_____   _____

Exercise 6

FIGHT AND FLIGHT COMBINED

Using your answers from **Exercise 4**, copy over the fighter's name and the worst way they fight on the top of this diagram. Using **Exercise 5**, copy over the flier's name and the worst way they fly on the bottom of this diagram.

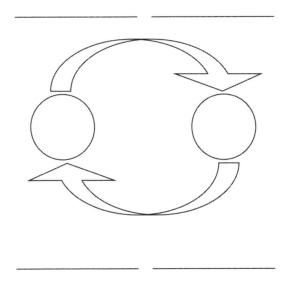

For many couples, these two reactions happen at the same time. They cause one another and go round and round in a vicious cycle.

Could this be true for you?   ❏ yes ❏ no

Exercise 7

THE HURT

If your partner fights, you probably have some hurt feelings. If you fight, your partner probably has some hurt feelings. Let's find a word for those hurt feelings. If you're the one who hurts, you'll know the word. If your partner is the one who hurts, try to put yourself in their shoes.

How strong is each of these feelings when your partner is fighting, or when your partner thinks that you are fighting?

	Don't feel this way		Moderately strong		Very strong
	0	1	2	3	4
Hurt	❑	❑	❑	❑	❑
Attacked	❑	❑	❑	❑	❑
Criticized	❑	❑	❑	❑	❑
Scared	❑	❑	❑	❑	❑
Inadequate	❑	❑	❑	❑	❑
Controlled	❑	❑	❑	❑	❑
Powerless	❑	❑	❑	❑	❑
Overwhelmed	❑	❑	❑	❑	❑
Smothered	❑	❑	❑	❑	❑
Unloved	❑	❑	❑	❑	❑
_____	❑	❑	❑	❑	❑

(add your own word)

Of your highest scores, which is the strongest feeling?

_____

Write the name of the person who hurts and the word for their deepest hurt. For instance "Carol feels attacked," or "Charlie feels criticized."

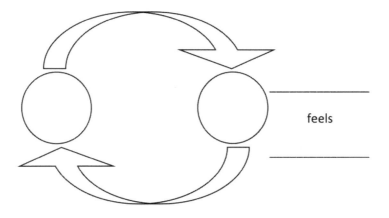

feels

Exercise 8

THE LONELINESS

If your partner flies, you probably have some lonely feeling. If you fly, your partner probably feels some lonely feeling. Let's find a word for that loneliness. If you're the one who's lonely, you'll know the word. If your partner is the one who's lonely, try to put yourself in their shoes.

How strong is each of these feelings when your partner flies, or thinks that you are flying?

	Don't feel this way		Moderately strong		Very strong
	0	1	2	3	4
Lonely	❏	❏	❏	❏	❏
Rejected	❏	❏	❏	❏	❏
Unwanted	❏	❏	❏	❏	❏
Betrayed	❏	❏	❏	❏	❏
Abandoned	❏	❏	❏	❏	❏
Dismissed	❏	❏	❏	❏	❏
Frustrated	❏	❏	❏	❏	❏
Helpless	❏	❏	❏	❏	❏
Insecure	❏	❏	❏	❏	❏
Anxious	❏	❏	❏	❏	❏
_____	❏	❏	❏	❏	❏

(add your own word)

Of your highest scores, which is the strongest feeling?

_____

Write the name of the person who feels lonely and the word for their deepest loneliness. For instance "Dan feels rejected," or "Darlene feels unwanted."

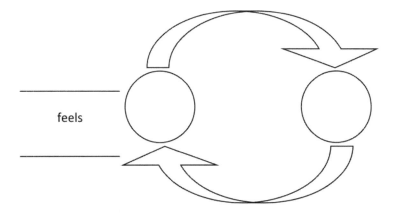

feels

Exercise 9
_____

HURT AND LONELINESS COMBINED

Using **Exercise 7** and **Exercise 8**, copy over each of your feelings onto the diagram below. One of you will be on one side of this diagram. The other person will be on the other side of this diagram.

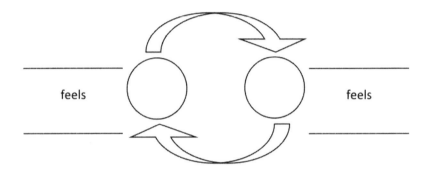

For many couples these two feelings happen at the same time. Each person's feeling leads to the other's feeling, and the two go round and round in a vicious cycle.

Could this be true for you?　　❑ yes　❑ no

Exercise 10

YOUR FEAR CYCLE

Go back to **Exercise 6**. Above the top arrow, and below the bottom arrow, write your answers to **Exercise 6.**

Go back to **Exercise 9**. By the circles on the right and left of the diagram below, write your answers to **Exercise 9.**

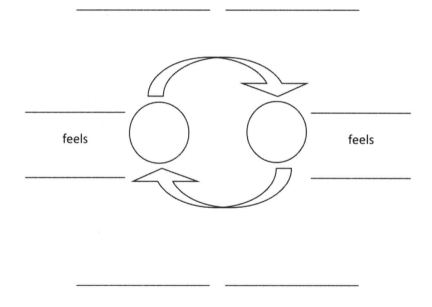

feels   feels

This is your fear cycle. It combines your fight or flight reactions and your hurt or lonely feelings.

Now skip to **Exercise 12.**

WHAT'S THE WORST?

If you just completed **Exercise 10**, skip this exercise and go to **Exercise 12**. This exercise is for couples who don't have the usual fight/flight pattern. The following questions will help you figure out your fear cycle:

1. When things are bad between you, what's the worst thing your partner does? On the diagram below, write their name and this worst thing they do above the top arrow.

2. When they do this, how does it make you feel? Write your name and this feeling on the right-hand circle.

3. When you feel this way, what is the worst thing you do? Write your name and your worst reaction below the bottom arrow.

4. When you react this way, what is the worst way your partner feels? Write their name and this feeling on the left-hand circle.

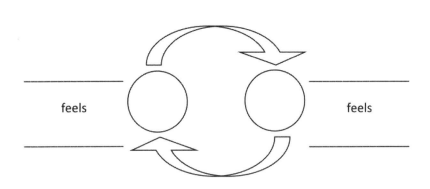

Exercise 12

DOES IT ALL CONNECT?

Using your diagram from **Exercise 10** or **Exercise 11**, read your cycle going clockwise.

Does each arrow lead to the feeling in the next circle?
     ❏ yes   ❏ no

Does each circle lead to the action on the next arrow?
     ❏ yes   ❏ no

Can you see the connections?
     ❏ yes   ❏ no

Does the whole cycle make sense?
     ❏ yes   ❏ no

If all your answers are yes, skip **Exercise 13** and go to **Exercise 14**.

If one or more of your answers is no, go to **Exercise 13**.

Exercise 13

WHAT IF IT DOESN'T CONNECT?

If it doesn't all connect, think about the connection that doesn't make sense.

Is the feeling in the circle the deepest feeling? Might there be deeper feelings? What might they be?

_____

What other feelings could possibly be caused by the arrow before that circle?

_____

What other feelings could possibly lead to the arrow after that circle?

_____

_____

Might these connections make sense for your partner even though they wouldn't make sense for you? What sense would it make for them?

_____

_____

Change the words on your diagram in **Exercise 10** or **Exercise 11** until all the links connect and the whole cycle makes sense.

Exercise 14

YOUR FOUR WORDS

Go back to **Exercise 10** or **Exercise 11**, and choose one word for each of the four places. If you've already written a single word, copy that word here. If you've written more than one word, choose the one that best captures the essence of all of them. Write that one word here.

Choose one action word for the top arrow_____

Choose one feeling word for the right-hand circle_____

Choose one action word for the bottom arrow_____

Choose one feeling word for the circle on the left _____

These are your four words. Together, they make your fear cycle.

This is what makes you miserable. It's what you need to change.

Exercise 15

IN YOUR CHILDHOOD,
DID YOU HAVE SIMILAR EXPERIENCES?

Almost everyone's fear cycle is rooted in their past, usually in their family upbringing. The following questions compare your fear cycle to your childhood experiences.

Did you have any parts of this fear cycle when you were growing up?

- Did you get the same treatment you get now (their arrow)?
  ❑ yes ❑ no

- Did you feel the same feeling you feel now (your circle)?
  ❑ yes ❑ no

- Did you react in the same way you react now (your arrow)?
  ❑ yes ❑ no

If all of your answers are **no**, now turn to **Exercise 16.**

If one or more of your answers is **yes**, write a few words about that. For instance, "Dad yelled," or "I missed my Mom," or "I got silent."

_____

_____

Could your childhood experiences have made you:

- More wary?   ❑ yes ❑ no

- More sensitive? ❑ yes ❑ no

- More reactive?   ❑ yes ❑ no

If yes, how? Write a few words about that. For instance, "I react very strongly to yelling," or "I'm very sensitive to people leaving."

_____

_____

Now skip to **Exercise 17**.

DID YOU HAVE THE OPPOSITE EXPERIENCES IN YOUR CHILDHOOD?

When you grew up, did you have the opposite experiences from the ones you are having now?

- Did you get the opposite treatment? (opposite of their arrow)
  ❑ yes ❑ no

- Did you have the opposite feelings? (opposite of your circle)
  ❑ yes ❑ no

- Did you have the opposite reaction? (opposite of your arrow)
  ❑ yes ❑ no

If one or more of your answers is **yes**, write a few words about that. For instance, "Dad was calm with me," or "I felt secure."

_____

_____

Could your childhood experiences have made you:

- More wary?   ❑ yes ❑ no

- More sensitive? ❑ yes ❑ no

- More reactive?   ❑ yes ❑ no

If yes, how? Write a few words about that. For instance, "I'm not accustomed to yelling," or "I have no experience with insecurity."

_____

_____

Now turn to **Exercise 17**.

Exercise 17
_____

DID YOUR PARTNER HAVE SIMILAR EXPERIENCES IN THEIR CHILDHOOD?

Now think about your partner's childhood. Compare your fear cycle to your partner's childhood. Did they have some of these same experiences when they were growing up?

- Did they get the same kind of treatment they get from you? (your arrow)

  ❏ yes ❏ no

- Did they feel this same kind of feeling? (their circle)

  ❏ yes ❏ no

- Did they react in the same kind of way? (their arrow)

  ❏ yes ❏ no

If all of your answers are **no**, turn to **Exercise 18** now.

If one or more of your answers is **yes**, write a few words about that. For instance, "His Dad yelled," or "She felt lonely," or "He got silent."

_____

_____

Could their childhood experiences have made them

- More wary?   ❏ yes ❏ no

- More sensitive? ❏ yes ❏ no

- More reactive?   ❏ yes ❏ no

If yes, how? Write a few words about that. For instance, "He reacts very strongly to yelling," or "She is very sensitive to people leaving."

_____

_____

Now skip to **Exercise 19**.

Exercise 18

DID YOUR PARTNER HAVE THE OPPOSITE EXPERIENCES IN THEIR CHILDHOOD?

When your partner grew up, did he or she have the opposite experiences from now?

- Did they get the opposite treatment?
    (opposite of your arrow)
    ❑ yes ❑ no

- Did they have the opposite feelings?
    (opposite of his or her circle)
    ❑ yes ❑ no

- Did they have the opposite reaction?
    (opposite of his or her arrow)
    ❑ yes ❑ no

If one or more of your answers is **yes**, write a few words about that. For instance, "His Dad was calm," or "Her Mom was always there."

_____

_____

Could their childhood experiences have made them:

- More wary?   ❑ yes ❑ no

- More sensitive?   ❑ yes ❑ no

- More reactive?   ❑ yes ❑ no

If yes, how? Write a few words about that. For instance, "He's not accustomed to yelling," or "She has no experience with insecurity."

_____

_____

Now turn to **Exercise 19**.

YOUR DREAM

No one wants their fear cycle. Every part of it is unpleasant.

Instead, think about what you DO want. What would you rather have? What are you yearning for instead? What's your dream?

From **Exercise 14**, copy your Four Words. Next to each word write its opposite.

_____	_____
(top arrow)	(opposite)
_____	_____
(right-hand circle)	(opposite)
_____	_____
(bottom arrow)	(opposite)
_____	_____
(left-hand circle)	(opposite)

Read your four opposites. Could one of these opposites be what you really want? Could something that combines a number of these opposites be what you really want?

On the line below, write your **dream**.

What I really want is to feel_____

_____

Exercise 20

YOUR PARTNER'S DREAM

Now do the same for your partner.

Think about what they want. What would they rather have in place of this fear cycle? What are they yearning for?

Go back to **Exercise 19** and read your four words and their opposites.

Could one of these opposites be what your partner really wants? Could something that combines a number of these opposites be what they really want?

On the line below, write your best guess for your partner's dream.

I think my partner really wants to feel_____

_____

LET YOUR DREAM GUIDE YOU

Your dream can guide you. It can show you what to do and what not to do. On each line copy over your entries from the earlier exercise. Then see if the advice here makes sense.

I should do things that lead to_____

(my dream, **Exercise 19**)

I shouldn't do things that lead to _____

(my feeling from **Exercise 14**)

If I want to feel_____

(my dream, **Exercise 19**)

I shouldn't do_____

(my fight or flight, **Exercise 6**)

Because that just leads to _____

(my feeling from **Exercise 14**)

Exercise 22

YOUR LOVE ARROWS

From **Exercise 6**, copy over what you wrote on your arrow. This is what you do in your fear cycle.

Write down a number of things that would be the opposite of that.

	1	2	3	4	5
_____	❑	❑	❑	❑	❑
_____	❑	❑	❑	❑	❑
_____	❑	❑	❑	❑	❑
_____	❑	❑	❑	❑	❑
_____	❑	❑	❑	❑	❑
_____	❑	❑	❑	❑	❑

From **Exercise 19**, look at your partner's dream. On your list of opposites above, how much would each make your partner feel their dream? Rate each. 1 is the least, 5 is the most.

Choose the one with the highest rating. If two or more have the same highest rating, choose the one that would most touch your partner's heart. That's your love arrow.

My love arrow is

Do this whenever you can.

Exercise 23
_____

THEIR LOVE ARROWS

From **Exercise 6**, copy over what you wrote on your partner's arrow. This is what they do in your fear cycle.

_____

Write down a number of things that would be the opposite of that.

	1	2	3	4	5
_____	❑	❑	❑	❑	❑
_____	❑	❑	❑	❑	❑
_____	❑	❑	❑	❑	❑
_____	❑	❑	❑	❑	❑
_____	❑	❑	❑	❑	❑
_____	❑	❑	❑	❑	❑

From **Exercise 19**, look at your dream. On your list of opposites above, how much would each make you feel your dream? Rate each. 1 is the least, 5 is the most.

Choose the one with the highest rating. If two or more have the same highest rating, choose the one that would most touch your heart. That's your partner's love arrow.

Their love arrow is

_____

Whenever they do this, let them know how much you like it.

Exercise 24

YOUR LOVE CYCLE

Now make a diagram of your love cycle. It's the opposite of your fear cycle. Your fear cycle has four negative words; your love cycle has four really positive words for this cycle.

By the circles on the right and left, copy over the dreams from **Exercise 19**. On the arrows on the top and bottom, copy over the love arrows from **Exercise 21** and **Exercise 22**. This is your love cycle

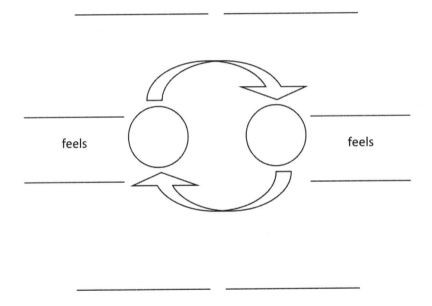

Your love cycle is very important for the two of you. Do it as much as possible.

It's the way to be happy together.

RESOURCES FOR GETTING PROFESSIONAL HELP

Many people benefit from having a professional help them repair their relationship. That's not a bad thing. In fact it can be a very good thing. Sure, if you can fix something yourself, you should. But if you can't fix it yourself, it's good to get help. Maybe give it a few months of trying on your own, but don't give it a few years. That's too long. If things aren't improving in a matter of months, it's probably wise to get professional help.

There are also certain situations where it might be wise to start with professional help right away. These include affairs, abuse, and addiction. These situations are really challenging, and a therapist's guidance is probably a good idea.

Below are some organizations that list therapists throughout the United States and the world. They can be a good starting point for whom to call. It's good to contact a number of different therapists so you can choose the one that feels the best to you.

One large database is Psychology Today. It lists therapists from many disciplines: psychologists, social workers, counselors, and marriage and family therapists. You can search by location and by specialty at psychologytoday.com

An equivalent listing for psychologists is maintained by the American Psychological Association. You can search psychologists by location and by specialty at locator.apa.org.

Each of the schools of therapy that Deborah and I have studied has their own directory of practitioners. Therapists trained by Terry Real practice Relational Empowerment Therapy. They are likely to be good at working with challenging situations. They're usually good at motivating reluctant partners. You can find a Relational Empowerment Therapist at terryreal.com/therapist-map.

Therapists trained by Dr. Harville Hendrix do Imago Relationship Therapy. They usually are very good at couples communication, and bringing to light the impact of each partner's childhood experiences. You can find an Imago Therapist at:
imagorelationships.org/pub/find-a-therapist

Therapists trained by Dr. Sue Johnson do Emotionally-Focused Therapy. They are usually very good at understanding and validating emotions, as well as unearthing the underlying attachment needs of each party. They are also particularly focused on cycles in relationships. You can find an Emotionally-Focused Therapist at:
iceeft.com/index.php/find-a-therapist

Therapists trained by Drs. John and Julie Gottman do Gottman Method Relationship Therapy. They are usually very good at explaining the scientific basis of a good relationship. They are good at using cognitive-behavioral interventions to help couples improve their situations. You can find a Gottman Method Relationship Therapist at:
gottman.com/couples/private-therapy

You are also welcome to contact us at The Woodsfellow Institute for Couples Therapy in Atlanta, GA. We do marriage counseling and relationship coaching, and we also are glad to make referrals to other therapists who may be able to help you. We wish you all the best as you work to improve your relationship. We wish you more love and happiness in your lives.

We can be reached at marriagehelpatlanta.com.

INDEX

A

Abandonment, 6, 14, 30, 77
  cycle, diagram, 38, 97, 104, 130, 137
  feeling, 6, 49–50, 83, 86
  trouble, 91–92
Abuse, 25
Acceptance/change, paradox, 143–144
Accommodation, 69
Accusation, 21
Actions, selection, 167
Addicts, 57
Adjustments, 143–144
Aesop, 131
Affairs, 57
Aggressiveness, 27
Agreed-upon saving/spending,
    compromise, 132
Alcoholics, 57
American Psychological Association,
    183
Amygdala, emotional center, 21
Anger, 21, 36, 54–55, 81, 127
  absence, 51
  apology, 49
  cycle, 77
    diagram, 33, 97, 104
    undoing, 66
  dialogue, 19
  dislike, 120
  feeling, 81–82

  getting angry, 22
  handling, process, 129–130
  impact, 6, 33–34
  increase, 34
  intensity, 65
  measurement, 121–122
  reduction, 66
"Ant and the Grasshopper, The"
    (Aesop), 131
Anxiety, 30
  cycle, diagram, 142
Appointments, making, 17
Arguments
  avoidance, perception, 14
  couple initiation, 53–54
  order, decision, 106–108
Arrow, shooting, 65
  action, opposition, 67
  avoidance, 67–68, 115
  cessation, 71
  change, 65–67, 75–76
  dislike, 113–114
  holding, love (equivalence), 69
  love arrow, exercise, 179–180
  response, change, 74–75
Attack
  feeling, 27
  perception, 15
Avoidance
  flying method, 23
  perspective, 8

Gratefulness, 114
Guilt, cycle (diagram), 41

H
Habit, breaking, 92
Harm
   fear, 6, 49
   impact, 6
Heart, 118–119
Hendrix, Harville, 100, 184
Hoarding, 143
House, background, 118
Human needs, absence, 25
Hurt
   basic fear, 25
   cycle, diagram, 36, 111, 135
   exercise, 158–159
   feelings, 27–28, 158
   loneliness, combination, 35–37
      exercise, 162
   partner feelings, 28–29
Hurt feelings, history, 81–83

I
Imago Relationship Therapy, 184
Imperfect relationships, lesson, 93
Inadequacy, feeling, 27
Incompatibility, belief, 5–7
Indignation, 50
Infidelity, 129
In-laws, 127
   blame, cycle (diagram), 133
   interaction, 132–134
Innocent victim, 50, 55, 72, 93
Insecurity, 30
   cycle, diagram, 131

Insensitivity, 26
Insights
   power, 61
   pursuit, error, 61–62
   strategy, 68
   usage, 94
Insults, cessation, 65
Intentions, 23, 47
   assumptions, 78
Intimidation, 52
   cycle, diagram, 97, 104
   feeling
      absence, 51
      impact, 89
   withdrawal, 79
Intolerance, feeling, 75
Issue, owning, 117

J
Johnson, Sue, 184
Jung, Carl, 127

K
Kindness, cycle (diagram), 105
Klein, Barry, 101

L
Lateness, cycle (diagram), 140
Leniency, cycle (diagram), 41, 135
Life, unpleasantness, 141
Listening, willingness, 115–116
Loneliness
   absence, cycle (diagram), 111
   cycle, diagram, 36, 39
   exercise, 160–161
   experience, 84

ABOUT THE AUTHORS

photo © Atwell Photography

David and Deborah Woodsfellow are the founders and directors of the Woodsfellow Institute for Couples in Atlanta, Georgia. The Woodsfellow Institute is dedicated to couples who want to enjoy life together, and therapists who want to learn more about couples therapy. The Woodsfellows have been training therapists to do couples therapy for fifteen years. Over 1,200 therapists have taken their couples therapy workshops, and over 200 therapists have taken their intensive sessions of months-long, small-group trainings.

The Woodsfellow Institute for Couples Therapy is an Approved Provider of Continuing Education by the American Psychological

Association, the Georgia Psychological Association, the Georgia Association of Marital and Family Therapists, and the Licensed Professional Counselors Association of Georgia.

David and Deborah have extensive training in Relational Empowerment Therapy, Scientifically-Based Relationship Therapy, Imago Therapy, Mars/Venus Counseling, and Emotionally-Focused Couples Therapy.

As a Licensed Psychologist, David has worked exclusively with couples for twenty-five years, doing over 25,000 hours of couples therapy. David has helped over 1,500 couples rebuild happier lives together. A Fellow of the Georgia Psychological Association, David has Master Certification in Relational Empowerment Therapy. He is also a Certified Imago Relationship Therapist and a Certified Mars/Venus Counselor.

David received his BA magna cum laude from Harvard College and his MA in Counseling Psychology from the University of California Santa Barbara. His PhD in clinical psychology was from Georgia State University and he did his clinical psychology internship at the Neuropsychiatric Institute, University of California Los Angeles School of Medicine.

As a Relationship Coach, Deborah works with couples and individuals who want to improve their relationships. She has been coaching couples for ten years, and co-teaching workshops for couples and for therapists for fifteen years. A former Navy Corpsman and Physician Assistant, Deborah received her Physician Associate degree from Emory University School of Medicine and her Masters in Public Health from Emory University School of Public Health.

David and Deborah live in Atlanta, Georgia. David is an avid cyclist who recently rode his recumbent trike across the United States. Deborah is a dog enthusiast who trains her standard poodles to be therapy dogs.